Praise for *It's More and Rainbo*

A positive and purposeful book with the occasional dollop of humour added throughout. Almost every sentence and paragraph needs highlighting for its ideas, provocation, or information. Ian's experience of growing up with homophobic bullying, and finding the courage it takes to come out, brings home the absolute need for every school to address LGBT+ identities as a core part of their approach to diversity, equality, inclusion, and belonging.

I wish had been given this book as a core text at the start of teaching. It would have been simultaneously enlightening and affirming of my values and passions within education. Furthermore, the explanations of terminology and the considered reasons for doing or not doing particular actions are very clear.

This is a brilliant book! I found it easy to read. A useful way to foster inclusion at any school or organisation that values all children and young people, outside or in.

Juliet Robertson, education consultant and author of
Blood Lines, Dirty Teaching,* and *Messy Maths

This book will be enormously helpful to those responsible for schools, whether as governor, school leader, or with local authority or MAT responsibilities. The issues around gender and identity are some of the most complex challenges facing schools today. Those issues are dealt with in a clear and measured analysis of every aspect. Ian Timbrell offers a coherent approach with guidelines for decisions and advice on best ways forward, all with sensitivity and always in the best interests of young people.

Mick Waters, educationalist and author

Ian has written a book that clearly comes from both his personal and political awareness. As a gay teacher who, like so many before him, had a torrid time at school – experiencing no positive mention of homosexuality and suffering bouts of homophobic bullying – he writes with passion and knowledge in the hope of making sure that another generation does not have to suffer as he did.

It is a very well-constructed how-to book for educators and anyone who is working in an organisation, taking the reader through clear steps that are not only LGBTQ+ friendly but explore and enable inclusivity.

The book is timely given the challenges we now face with the right wing particularly in America but also here in the UK, challenging the human rights of trans people. The book takes the reader on a journey to discover the myriad of reasons why the work is necessary, the footnotes and resources alone are compelling. The discussion of emotional suffering and scarring leading to unfulfilled potential makes clear to the uninitiated the crucialness of the work.

Ian uses a compassionate tone, indicating that we all need to learn – that knowing how defamatory language, lack of representation and silence has a negative effect, not only on young people who know they are LGBT+ or who are beginning to think they might be, but on everyone. Ignorance leads to prejudice, and it is every teacher and employer's job to make sure that every student and staff member is safe and in a position where they can be seen as who they are.

It's More Than Flags and Rainbows is a clever title, indicating as it does that superficial signalling is not sufficient. Ian takes care to guide us through small steps that have a fair chance of success. Then leads us on slowly to deeper changes that will affect the school or organisational culture and its curriculum or policies.

Throughout he offers examples of resources and reminds us to take care of ourselves and find named allies to support us. So check out the footnotes and the resources at the back and you will have a companion and guide to the crucial work of ensuring that your organisation recognises and celebrates each and every person in it.

**Sue Sanders, she/her, professor emeritus, CEO of Schools OUT,
co-founder of UK LGBT+ History Month**

It's More Than Flags and Rainbows offers practical and actionable insights for education professionals interested in LGBTQ+ diversity and inclusion. It explores key themes with nuance and does not shy away from the more difficult conversations that need to be had in order to create meaningful inclusion beyond flags and rainbows. Ian shares his lived experience as a gay man, his practical knowledge as a former teacher, and his expertise as an LGBTQ+ diversity and inclusion consultant to create a thought-provoking guide for educators. This book is a great and timely addition to the field of LGBTQ+ inclusive education!

Jo Brassington and Dr Adam Brett, founders and hosts of Pride & Progress

IT'S MORE THAN
FLAGS AND
RAINBOWS

Getting LGBTQ+ provision right in schools

Ian Timbrell

independent
thinking press

First published by
Independent Thinking Press
Crown Buildings, Bancyfelin, Carmarthen, Wales, SA33 5ND, UK
www.independentthinkingpress.com

and

Independent Thinking Press
PO Box 2223, Williston, VT 05495, USA
www.crownhousepublishing.com

Independent Thinking Press is an imprint of Crown House Publishing Ltd.

EU GPSR Authorised Representative
Appointed EU Representative: Easy Access System Europe Oü, 16879218
Address: Mustamäe tee 50, 10621, Tallinn, Estonia
Contact Details: gpsr.requests@easproject.com, +358 40 500 3575

Edited by Ian Gilbert.

British Library of Cataloguing-in-Publication Data

A catalogue entry for this book is available from the British Library.

Print ISBN: 978-178135428-5
Mobi ISBN: 978-178135436-0
ePub ISBN: 978-178135437-7
ePDF ISBN: 978-178135438-4

LCCN 2025932067

Printed in the UK by
CPi, Antony Rowe, Chippenham, Wiltshire

Acknowledgements

Thank you to my husband, Rhys, who gave me the confidence to take a step away from teaching and to dive headfirst into the world of LGBTQ+ inclusion and wider diversity education and training. I could never have done it without your support, and I thank you every day.

To my son, who is part of the reason for writing this book. I do this book for you. To make the world you are growing up in more accepting, no matter who you grow up to be.

To my two head teachers during my time teaching, Kate Evans and Sarah Jones. You both supported my dreams and gave me a kick up the ass when needed but never stopped believing in me.

To Jo Brassington and Adam Brett from Pride & Progress, Catrina Lowri from Neuroteachers, and Cat Wildman from Powered by Diversity – your work in inclusive spaces inspired me so much in my early days of this work, and it has been amazing to get to know you all.

To my family, but particularly my parents, Carl and Sue, my sisters, Karen and Rachel, and my best friend, Marc, who put up with my nonsense and are continually supportive.

And, finally, to Ian Gilbert, who saw something in me and gave me an opportunity which led to the creation of this book.

I could not have done this without you all, and I will be eternally grateful.

Contents

Introduction

. . . .

'It's wacky! It's fun! It's cr-a-a-a-zy! It's outrageous! Fun House, it's a whole lot of fun ...'

If you can finish that line, then you are probably around my age (and if you aren't, I urge you to check it out on YouTube). This is from the gameshow *Fun House* with the incomparable Pat Sharp. In typical 1980s and 1990s kids TV show fashion, there was complete chaos jammed into a 30-minute show. From searching around the house for tags and labels to finishing with a go-kart race, it was a cultural phenomenon. But the show (however amazing) is not the point here.

Ten-year-old me had the biggest celebrity crush on the presenter Pat Sharp and his long golden mullet. All I wanted to do was brush his hair and drive around in a go-kart together (what dreams!). But why didn't anyone else talk about him in this way? Why were they all fixated on the leotard-clad blonde twins? Sure, they were pretty, but not compared to my Pat.

It didn't matter to me at the time, and I don't remember being bothered by feeling different to other people. But the lack of conversation around what I was experiencing, and an absence of certain words from the school vocabulary, meant that I was oblivious as to why I was feeling that way. As I got older, I just assumed that it was something that would eventually go away.

I loved primary school, which I remember as a happy, energetic, and supportive environment. But unbeknownst to us at the time, this support was selective and didn't actually include everyone. There were large proportions of our population missing from the curriculum. Where were the people who felt like I did? Although I didn't know it, these people existed. But where were they?

The end of Year 6 came, and I began a new adventure in secondary school. And that is where everything changed. I was introduced to a new word: gay. But this wasn't through conversation or education; it was through bullying. These school experiences set me on course for where I am today. A life of highs and lows but, most of all, an exploration of identity and acceptance that is still going on 30 years later.

....

Why More Than Flags and Rainbows?

Get your flags and rainbows ready, give everyone rainbow lanyards, hold a Pride event, and BANG you have an inclusive school. Right?

This is what we see in many areas of society, especially around Pride Month. Businesses change their logos to rainbow versions, shop windows suddenly become 'rainbowfied', and there is a lot of rainbow merchandise for sale in stores. But this is not just businesses; schools are guilty of it too. Whether we are talking about a few assemblies in LGBT+ History Month, a solitary lesson in Black History Month, or buying some inclusive books and putting them in a box in the library, many people try to improve inclusivity from good intentions. Although it should not be the motivation behind these actions, schools sometimes feel they must do these things or do them because it makes them look good. This is what we would call virtue signalling and, unfortunately, it is very prevalent in education and society (do not get me started on social media). This is what I want to help you to avoid. Instead, what I want you to achieve is the beginning of long-term and meaningful change for a genuine purpose. I want to help you plan an approach which will help every child to feel safe, seen, and supported.

I am not saying you should not wear rainbow lanyards or do one-off lessons or assemblies, but these activities are going to have limited impact in the long term without wider cultural and curriculum change. If lessons or assemblies are isolated and not combined with a comprehensively inclusive curriculum, there is a risk that minorities are viewed as separate to the rest of society, as something other-than, or (and I hate to say the word) as not normal. We need to carefully consider how we build a curriculum where the diversity of our world is recognised, and diverse groups are viewed as integrated rather than separate entities within communities.

Celebrating and discussing differences are important, but so too are identifying our similarities and the values and attitudes that we share in common.

You might have already guessed why I named this book It's *More Than Flags and Rainbows,* but it does not come from an imaginary place. After visiting a school covered in rainbow flags and lanyards, but where the pupils felt unsafe and unrepresented, I had a conversation with the wonderful Ian Gilbert (author of *The Little Book of Thunks* and many more[1]) about diversity education in schools. This led to a discussion about how to create an approach where we avoid virtue signalling and instead develop real and meaningful change. I would like to think that no one sets out to tick a diversity box, but sometimes people do not know where to start and so go for the obvious visual symbols. And if that is you, I would just like to say that you should not feel guilty about it; these visual symbols and one-off events are important. But in this book we will be delving much deeper and combining these visual and individual events with more comprehensive approaches to create lasting change.

Although the focus of this book will be on LGBTQ+ diversity and inclusion, we will also be exploring wider diversity. No one group is more important than any other, and while specific discussion points and considerations are needed for LGBTQ+ pupils, many of the principles in this book are applicable to most areas of diversity.

How to use this book

So, who are you, and is this book right for you? Whether you are a head teacher, teacher, pastoral lead, or simply someone passionate about LGBTQ+ inclusion and diversity in schools, I have written this book with you in mind. It offers practical, actionable insights for all the education community, acknowledging that how you apply these steps may differ depending on your role. You may rely on support from various colleagues or departments but, ultimately, this book will equip you to help foster a more inclusive and supportive school environment.

---

1   I. Gilbert, *The Little Book of Thunks: 260 Questions to Make Your Brain Go Ouch!* (Carmarthen: Crown House Publishing, 2007).

At the beginning of every chapter is a vignette from my life story. I decided to include these as they not only provide context about how I arrived at my ideas, but they also demonstrate how many of the issues I am trying to tackle in this book appear in real life. Some of these episodes are difficult for me to talk about, but in a strange way, it was quite cathartic to write them down. I thank you for reading my story and getting to know me a bit better; it is a privilege to be able to share these events with you.

When writing this book, I wanted to describe a journey through improving the diversity and inclusion of a school because some people might not know where to start. You may decide to read this book from beginning to end or you might dip in and out. There is no one-size-fits-all approach. You must do what works for you and your school community. Whether that is taking individual chapters and adapting them to your setting or moving through the chapters incrementally, I hope you find the book useful and that it enhances your level of knowledge and confidence in improving diversity and inclusion.

First, we all need to have a common understanding of the words we will be using. In Chapter 1, you will learn the meaning behind LGBTQ+ concepts and terminology. I will pick apart some of the more complex issues, such as the word 'queer', and consider what exactly people are saying about transgender identities in schools. With this information, you will be far better equipped to discuss LGBTQ+ inclusion with your pupils and staff and ensure that the education you are delivering is accurate. You might already be wondering why I am using LGBTQ+ and not one of the plethora of other initialisms; do not panic, this will also be covered in Chapter 1.

In Chapters 2 and 3, you will explore where you are as a school community and how to create an action plan based on your findings. It can be very tempting to skip this step and go straight to doing (brace yourself for my favourite phrase) 'things and stuff', but this often results in surface-level changes or virtue signalling. I want to make sure you plan for long-term and sustainable change.

In the rest of the book, you will discover many ideas for the next steps that you and your school community can take. You may decide to read all these chapters before starting or just refer to the ones that are included in your action plan.

But before we begin, we need to explore why this work is necessary.

Why the DEIB?

I find it remarkable that in education, we have to justify our decision to improve diversity, equity, inclusion, and belonging (DEIB). I am sure you would agree that most educators come into teaching for more than just a job; they do so to make a difference. This might sound trite, but it is true; I do not think many people enter teaching because of the money or hours. So, it should be no surprise that teachers want to do the best for their pupils, especially those who are facing discrimination, or prejudice, or experiencing additional challenges in their lives.

We are in a challenging time for DEIB, where decisions made by schools are increasingly questioned on social media, in the media, and even in person, particularly regarding LGBTQ+ work. Accusations of age-inappropriate teaching, indoctrination, and grooming are prevalent on certain platforms, but these concerns are usually voiced by a minority only. It is easy for people to be misled by online echo chambers, but these views do not reflect the broader reality of what the wider population think or believe. The harsh comments online are often the work of keyboard warriors, and they rarely have a significant impact in real life. In the schools where I have worked, I have found overwhelmingly supportive communities. When challenges have arisen from individual families, they are typically rooted in misinformation or a lack of transparency from the school. In contrast to what some people would have you believe on social media, when you engage with your school community directly, rather than against it, any pushback you encounter will typically be limited to a small number of individuals.

I do not want to suggest that everything will always go smoothly and there will never be any challenges. You may very well receive criticism, pushback, or worse, and while this is mentally and emotionally demanding, I hope you have a team around you that can provide the support you need to continue the mission that you know is right. We will explore working with parents and the community in Chapter 8 to hopefully help you avoid these difficulties, but I will also give you some tools and strategies should there be disagreement or conflict between home and school.

Throughout this book, you will hear my own personal reasons for wanting to improve diversity and inclusion. However, my desire to improve the world is also rooted in the experiences of many others. There is plenty of evidence for why we should improve diversity and inclusion, which can generally be grouped into two areas: legal and moral.

The legal bit

The Equality Act 2010 brought together over 100 pieces of legislation to improve equity and reduce inequality in the UK. In the Act, there are nine protected characteristics: age, disability, gender reassignment, marriage and civil partnership, pregnancy and maternity, race, religion or belief, sex, and sexual orientation.[2] It is important to note that gender is not a protected characteristic in the UK. I will discuss sex and gender, and what this distinction means, in Chapter 1.

This book focuses on LGBTQ+ inclusion from a UK perspective, but it is relevant to other countries as well. Although the United States lacks a federal law mandating as many aspects of equality as the UK, several states have their own protections in place. In the United States, there have been attempts to create legislation which grants protections to LGBTQ+ people, particularly in the workplace, such as H.R.5.[3] However, these protections have not yet become law. In Australia, LGBTQ+ individuals are generally protected under the Sex Discrimination Act 1984, which includes gender as a protected characteristic in addition to sex.[4] While equality legislation varies across countries, this book addresses universal principles that can be adapted to different legal contexts.

---

2   See https://www.legislation.gov.uk/ukpga/2010/15/section/4.
3   See Congress.gov, H.R.5 – 116th Congress (2019–2020): Equality Act (20 May 2019). Available at: https://www.congress.gov/116/bills/hr5/BILLS-116hr5rfs.pdf.
4   See https://www.legislation.gov.au/C2004A02868/latest/text.

The moral bit

As you go through this book, you will be introduced to my story and what I went through in school and afterwards. But this is about more than me. This is about making every child, young person, and adult in our schools and our communities feel safe, seen, and supported.

The words *safe*, *seen*, and *supported* are commonly used to describe how to protect young people and children from harm and abuse. If young people have to hide who they are, or are made to feel less than 'normal', or are bullied for their identity, or do not get the education they need, they are not safe. If people do not see or learn about other people who are different to them, they will inevitably develop misconceptions or even prejudices. Coming out can be challenging for young people and their families, and if they are not supported, this can lead to isolation and mental-health challenges.

The statistics in this section may be difficult to read, but everyone involved should understand that DEIB work is about the mental health and well-being of young people. It is also important to recognise that when school ends, people's educational experiences continue to impact their work and personal life. This means that, although this book is focused on education, your work in schools will help to shape the adult citizens of tomorrow.

The following information comes from several sources:

✚ *Positive Futures: How Supporting LGBT+ Young People Enables Them to Thrive in Adulthood*, a report by the charity Just Like Us, which surveyed the experiences of 3,695 18- to 25-year-olds from across the UK in 2023.[5]

✚ *Growing up LGBT+: The Impact of School, Home and Coronavirus on LGBT+ Young People*, another report by Just

---

5 Just Like Us, *Positive Futures: How Supporting LGBT+ Young People Enables Them to Thrive in Adulthood* (2023). Available at: https://www.justlikeus.org/wp-content/uploads/2023/05/Positive-Futures-report-by-Just-Like-Us-compressed-for-mobile.pdf.

Like Us, which surveyed secondary school pupils in the UK in 2021.[6]

✚ The Trevor Project's *2023 U.S. National Survey on the Mental Health of LGBTQ Young People*, which gathered the experiences of more than 28,000 LGBTQ young people aged 13 to 24 across the United States in 2023.[7]

I urge you to take care of your own well-being if the following statistics are triggering for you. Based on my own experiences in school, this information was emotionally challenging to read and even more difficult to write.

Safe

Between 30% and 50% of LGBTQ+ young people are likely to have experienced bullying, with the data from previous years suggesting that this picture is not improving.

LGBTQ+ pupils are three times more likely to experience sexual harassment (7% of LGBT+ pupils have experienced unwanted sexual touching, including 12% of bisexual girls, compared to 2% of their non-LGBTQ+ peers).

Data from across the world indicate that around 41% of LGBTQ+ young people seriously consider attempting suicide each year, including roughly half of transgender and non-binary youth. This statistic is even higher for Black, transgender, and non-binary people, with up to 58% seriously considering suicide.

Seen

Some 74% of LGBT+ pupils who have never received positive messaging from their school about being LGBT+ have contemplated suicide. However, this rate decreases when schools offer strong positive messaging about being LGBT+.

---

6 Just Like Us, *Growing Up LGBT+: The Impact of School, Home and Coronavirus on LGBT+ Young People* (2021). Available at: https://www.justlikeus.org/wp-content/uploads/2021/11/Just-Like-Us-2021-report-Growing-Up-LGBT.pdf.
7 The Trevor Project, *2023 U.S. National Survey on the Mental Health of LGBTQ Young People* (2023). Available at: https://www.thetrevorproject.org/survey-2023/assets/static/05_TREVOR05_2023survey.pdf.

In the UK and United States, only around 40% of LGBT+ primary and secondary school staff are out to their pupils, signalling that most LGBT+ teachers feel forced into hiding who they are, their families, or who they are married to while they are at work.

Supported

Around 15% of LGBTQ+ survey respondents knew they were LGBT+ before they were 11. This means that this is not a secondary school issue; teachers of all age groups should be considering how they support LGBTQ+ children and young people.

LGBTQ+ young people are twice as likely to experience depression, anxiety, and panic attacks as well as to feel lonely and worry about their mental health on a daily basis.

It is very clear from this data that we still have not cracked LGBTQ+ inclusion, but why are we in this situation, and what can we do about it?

Heteronormativity

After becoming engaged, I was excitedly searching for wedding venues. The first one I looked at was a beautiful, converted barn with incredible views. When I contacted the owner, I was presented with a form which asked for two names: the 'bride' and the 'groom'. Now, for most people, this would not be an issue, and you may be wondering why we did not just throw our names into the fields regardless of what it said, but why should we? If you are a same-sex couple, who goes in the bride slot?

I immediately emailed the venue which responded swiftly – they were absolutely mortified. Within days, the website had been changed to 'Details for the happy couple'. This instance was not an aggression or a deliberate attempt to be prejudiced, but a classic case of an assumption being made that every couple contacting them would be straight, and reminds same-sex couples that they are different to most of society.

Studies from around the world show that between 90% and 97% of people identify as straight,[8] and so it is no wonder that our society is designed for straight people. When you add in the recent history of equal rights, it is no surprise either that our education system has only lately started to reflect the diverse make-up of relationships. The assumption that most people are straight is called heteronormativity and is one of the reasons that LGB+[9] people feel under-represented.

Take children's films. How many films before 2020 featured same-sex parents? How many books in schools include same-sex families as just part of the story without being a teaching point? This results in an impression that being straight is 'normal' and everything outside of that is not. But what about children who have two mums, are fostered or adopted, or are part of the wonderful diversity of families? If they never see families that look like theirs, then what message is society giving to them? It is the same when it comes to discussions around relationships. If in sex education in secondary school, teachers only ever talk about sexual intercourse between a man and a woman, LGB+ pupils may never receive sex education that is relevant to them. This is particularly problematic when sex education is solely focused on reproduction. And, let us be honest, the vast majority of times that consenting adults have sex is not for conception.

Tackling heteronormativity is not about banning pictures of straight couples or making every lesson incorporate LGBTQ+ identities but making sure that the curriculum and wider school environment is representative of all pupils and families.

It can be difficult to let go of this heteronormative view of the world as it can be very ingrained, and often people need to go through a process of 'unlearning' to consider a curriculum outside of their immediate expertise. Moreover, being LGBTQ+ does not make you immune to heteronormativity. As a gay man, I still make assumptions about people's relationships, and my view of the world is still built from a society that is primarily made for straight couples.

---

8 Office for National Statistics, Sexual Orientation, England and Wales, Census 2021 (6 January 2023). Available at: https://www.ons.gov.uk/peoplepopulationandcommunity/culturalidentity/sexuality/bulletins/sexualorientationenglandandwales/census2021; https://www.statista.com/statistics/1270166/lgbt-identification-worldwide.
9 In Chapter 1, I will explain why I have used LGB+ here and not LGBT+ or LGBTQ+.

You do not know what you do not know

Before you begin your journey, I want you to reflect on your own experiences of LGBTQ+ inclusion, what you understand about it, and what is unknown or unfamiliar territory.

Think about what your education was like in school. Did you get taught what LGBTQ+ means? Did you learn about LGBTQ+ role models? Did you read books with two mums or dads or LGBTQ+ characters in them? For most people, the answer is a resounding no. I would like you to sit with that for a moment and consider why that is.

As you are reading this, you may very well be one of the many teachers or school leaders who might have inklings about where to start or what to do, but you may also be one of the many who does not know where to begin. I want you to take the pressure off yourself because there is a very clear reason why you do not know or are unsure – and it is most likely not your fault.

The history of LGBTQ+ rights

To help you understand why our society has not yet achieved true equality, we need to jump back in time. The history of LGBTQ+ inclusion is an interesting one, especially when looking at gay rights in particular.

Contrary to many people's beliefs, various cultures throughout history have embraced homosexuality and gender diversity. For example, the ancient Greeks did not have a word for homosexuality in the way that we describe it, and there were many different views on same-sex relationships.[10]

But times changed, and across the globe, often coupled with colonialism, laws criminalising homosexuality were introduced. These

---

10 T. K. Hubbard, Historical Views of Homosexuality: Ancient Greece, *Oxford Research Encyclopedia of Politics* (2020). Available at: https://oxfordre.com/politics/display/10.1093/acrefore/9780190228637.001.0001/acrefore-9780190228637-e-1242.

could dramatically change a country's perspective on sexuality and gender, restricting many viewpoints (often through draconian laws) to more 'Western' or 'conservative' views. Although we may think about colonialism existing in the past, some of these laws are still in place, with more than 10 countries still imposing the death penalty for being LGBT+, with post-colonial countries being far more likely to persecute homosexuality.[11]

When people ask why we still need Pride events or why we do not have straight Pride, ask them, in which countries you can be imprisoned or lose your life because you are straight?

Can you 'catch' being lesbian or gay?

In the UK, although we now have equality for LGBT people in law, this is a relatively recent development, and society is still adapting to these changes.

Section 28 of the Local Government Act 1988 came into effect during Margaret Thatcher's premiership. It stated that a local authority 'shall not intentionally promote homosexuality or publish material with the intention of promoting homosexuality' or 'promote the teaching in any maintained school of the acceptability of homosexuality as a pretended family relationship'.[12]

When we look at the language of the Act, it gives us a good idea of what life was like for many LGBTQ+ people at this time. It prohibits homosexuality being 'promoted', which seems to suggest that you can 'catch' being lesbian or gay, or that reading books with same-sex parents will somehow 'convert' children. This is, of course, utter rubbish. I was born gay. I just did not discover who I was until later because (in part due to this law) I was led to believe that everyone was straight and that it was the 'norm'.

Section 28 had a devastating impact on the growing LGBT equality movement, leading to the closure of a large number of LGBT pupil

---

11 E. Han and J. O'Mahoney, British Colonialism and the Criminalization of Homosexuality, *Cambridge Review of International Affairs*, 27(2) (2014), 268–288. https://doi.org/10.1080/09557571.2013.867298.
12 See https://www.legislation.gov.uk/ukpga/1988/9/section/28.

support groups.[13] It also scaremongered schools into not discussing any LGBT relationships in the classroom and essentially 'straight-washed' the education system. Even though there were openly gay people in the media and local communities, generally schools did not discuss them, and the Act denied this visibility, creating a climate of negativity and fear.[14] This law (which no local authority was ever prosecuted under because it was so unworkable) led to many people, like me, not even knowing that other LGBT people existed until much later in life.

Now, when someone like Sir Ian McKellen campaigns for something, you need to take note, and that is exactly what happened. There were campaigns against Section 28 from the start. Around the UK, there were many protests and marches using the slogan 'Stop the Clause', and campaigners such as McKellen lobbied for Section 28 to be repealed. The irony, of course, is that what many viewed as a culture war machine for gaining votes by the then Conservative government actually inspired one of the fastest growing civil rights movements in history. With rapidly changing views towards homosexuality, the law was repealed in Scotland in 2000 in one of the first acts of the new Scottish Parliament. It was repealed in the rest of the UK in 2003. But we have to consider that this is only 22 years prior to the writing of this book. Most teachers and parents will have been schooled at a time when Section 28 was in force, and inevitably it will have shaped their views on LGBTQ+ inclusion and rights.

The impact of history

You may be wondering how an Act of Parliament that was repealed over two decades ago is still having an impact in the UK today. But this is where we come back to the original point: you do not know what you do not know. I have worked with lots of teachers and school leaders who are still dealing with the mental-health implications of having to hide their identity for so long. It also means that

---

13 Knitting Circle, Section 28 Gleanings (1989). Available at: https://web.archive.org/web/20070818063344/http://www.knittingcircle.org.uk/gleanings2889.html.

14 V. Iglikowski-Broad, Section 28: Impact, Fightback and Repeal, *National Archives* (2023). Available at: https://beta.nationalarchives.gov.uk/explore-the-collection/stories/section-28-impact-fightback-repeal. See also Just Like Us, *Positive Futures*.

most teachers and school leaders have never themselves experienced what an inclusive LGBTQ+ education looks like or know what it should contain.

And so, when beginning this journey, it will be helpful for you to accept that there are some things outside of your immediate area of expertise and knowledge – and, for now, that is fine. But, from here on, I would ask you to carefully consider how you can use external and internal voices to support you to shape an approach to improving LGBTQ+ inclusion and fill in those gaps that were created by society through oppressive measures such as Section 28.

So, what can you do?

Improving the lives of LGBTQ+ young people is not an impossible task. Although the data may appear dire, the statistics also show that when LGBTQ+ young people are in a supportive environment, their mental health and well-being improves significantly. Through the principles of being safe, seen, and supported, you can make sure that young people get the education and environment they need to flourish.

As someone whose time in school was far from being safe, seen, and supported, I am personally grateful for you taking this step to making a difference to so many children, young people, and families.

Chapter 1

What the LGBTQIA+! Vocabulary, Language, and Concepts

L ittle did I know that my life, which was previously full of Pat Sharp and *ThunderCats*, would be so different in secondary school. Starting Year 7 was exciting, daunting, and overwhelming, but like many Year 7s, I was looking forward to it. I went to one of the biggest secondary schools in the country; it was spread over three sites and felt like a small town. I grew up in Bridgend, South Wales, which had a huge ex-mining and rugby culture. I was very sporty and academic, so I should have fitted right in. But there was one problem: no matter what I was good at, I was the wrong sort of boy.

My parents were eager for me to begin secondary school and bought me a brand new blazer to wear on my first day. Unfortunately for me, blazers were optional and not one other person wore one. I soon became known as 'blazer boy'. (Ian Eagleton, if you're reading this, let's write a book together called *Blazer Boy*; I can only imagine his superpowers and the adventures he will go on.) This was my first experience of name-calling in school, and as anyone who has experienced it knows, it is always more unpleasant than it seems. There was a huge culture of 'banter', and this constant ribbing of one another covered up a nasty undercurrent that was part of the fabric of the school. So many pupils were either subject to or perpetrators of this banter that it was often impossible to tell what was good-natured ribbing and what was simply an insult.

Within a few weeks of starting school, I learned a new word: gay. This word was used as a jeer to taunt and bully me. At first it was a small group of boys in my year group, but soon pupils in other year groups were using it too. I have no idea why I was targeted. I certainly didn't ever use or identify with the word at that time. I have often wondered what it was they saw in me that meant gay was applicable to me. Was it that I was a bit camp? Was it because I was blonde, quiet, and a bit of a geek, so I was an easy target? Some may say that 'You can always tell,' but if that was true then all gay kids would be bullied (which they aren't, although they are more likely to be) and no one who isn't gay would be bullied using that word (which isn't the case). At this time, the word 'gay' was prevalent as an insult, and I certainly wasn't the only one being tormented by its use.

Sadly, the insults and bullying did not stop at the word 'gay'. In Year 7 alone, I was also called names such as 'queer', 'faggot', and 'poof'. I was spat at. Rumours were spread about me. I had my bag stolen. I went from being a kid who loved school to someone who dreaded every moment between lessons. For the first time in school, I became silly; I started messing around and being the class clown. But who wouldn't when you would do anything you could to cheer yourself up? As a primary teacher for 17 years, I often saw pupils I had taught transform in this way at secondary school and would wonder what had happened to make them go so off the rails. But in the whole of Year 7, no one ever thought to check if I was okay or to question why I was so different from when I was at primary school. I still feel today that I was just a number, just a statistic, and just seen en masse rather than as an individual who needed nurture and support.

The bullying went on for a year, and by Year 8 I'd had enough. I went to the deputy head teacher and told him everything: what had happened, who did it, where and when. And then he said the immortal words that I will never forget: 'Just fit in like everyone else and the bullying will go away.' When I tell people this, I get a range of responses from shock to disgust to disbelief. But I did exactly what he said. After all, this was the person who was supposed to be responsible for ensuring my well-being, so why wouldn't I do what he advised?

I started copying what everyone else wore. I pretended to like certain music. I pretended to like certain people. I pretended to like certain TV shows. All to hide. All to pretend that I was someone I was not. I began to lead a double life where home-Ian and school-Ian were two completely different people. At home I watched *Star Trek*. In school I spoke about sports. At home I liked 1990s pop and boybands. In school I liked indie bands. At home I thought about the handsome boys in my year group. In school I had girlfriend after girlfriend.

And did the bullying go away? Of course it didn't. The name-calling continued; I just stopped telling people about it. Perhaps if the other pupils had understood what it meant to be gay, and the school had a clear strategy on bullying and a culture of care and empathy, then the next six years of school wouldn't have been the hellscape that it was. And perhaps I wouldn't be experiencing the anxiety and depression I still grapple with today.

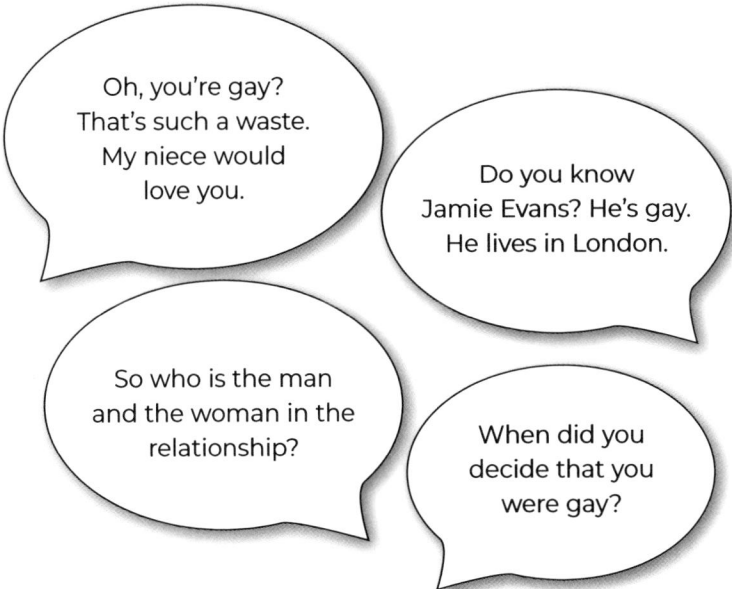

. . . .

Oh, you're gay? That's such a waste. My niece would love you.

Do you know Jamie Evans? He's gay. He lives in London.

So who is the man and the woman in the relationship?

When did you decide that you were gay?

As a consequence of the heteronormativity that I described in the Introduction, there are many misconceptions about being LGBTQ+. I have heard all the phrases listed above in the last few years. Now, please do not feel bad if you have said any of these things; I am sure you did not mean to cause any offence. Equally, no one who said these things to me was trying to be rude. But, inadvertently, these types of comment make LGBTQ+ people feel excluded and that something about them is not (and, as you will see, I hate using the word) 'normal'. They all show misconceptions and a lack of understanding about being gay. As you consider these remarks, let me ask you to think about some facts.

+ I have got a husband and a son. I am hardworking. I have lots of friends. Why is my life a waste because I am gay?

+ There are around 800 million gay men in the world. We do not all meet on a Monday evening for the Gay Men's Committee. It is true that the LGBTQ+ community is often tight-knit in some areas and people have things in common, but we do not all know each other, and we are not all the same.

+ I am a man. My partner is a man. What do you mean 'who is the woman'? You are either asking about our sexual positions (wildly inappropriate) or you are trying to make us into a straight couple, which we are not.

+ Honey, I have always been gay. Did you not read the Introduction and my story about Pat Sharp? LGBTQ+ people are born, not made.

The important thing in life is that people reflect on what they say and consider how it might inadvertently affect the other person. This includes me. I have definitely said things in my past that I should not have, and I absolutely said things earlier in my life that would be unacceptable now. Most of us do not choose to hurt people or to make them feel less than with the words we use, but no one is an expert on everything and so everyone needs to continually educate themselves on words and concepts that are not currently part of their vernacular. The words we use are not static; their meanings are fluid and shaped by societal context, personal experiences, and cultural influences. Words that were acceptable in the past might not be acceptable today or in the future. We need to build a society where it is okay to make mistakes. And if you do make a slip-up, just apologise, learn, and move on. We do not need drama.

Even reading the introduction to this chapter may leave you with questions about specific words or phrases. Please do not feel alone; you are definitely not. The evolution of language can leave some people feeling left behind or out of touch (in the same way that conversing with teenagers can sometimes feel like talking to someone using a completely different version of the English language). But I want to reassure you that no one holds all the knowledge about our lexicon. The important point is not to understand every word that people utter, but to build a culture where it is acceptable, even encouraged, for people to ask questions when they hear an unfamiliar word or phrase.

In this chapter, we will explore some linguistic concepts, including what familiar words and phrases mean, why a common understanding of language is so important, and tackle some of the myths that perpetuate in education and DEIB circles.

More labels than a label-maker

Some of the questions I have heard repeatedly since I started talking to more people about LGBTQ+ equality include: why does everyone seemingly need a label, why do we still need the letters, why are there so many combinations, and why are people still talking about LGBTQ+ identities so much? After all, in an increasing number of countries, LGBTQ+ people can get married and hold hands in the street – what more do we bloody well want?

It all comes down to the difference between legal and societal equality. It is true that just like a straight man in the UK, I can get married, my employment rights are protected, and I can adopt a child as part of a same-sex couple. All that progress is incredible and a testament to the work of the activists in this area. However, how many straight people have been heckled in the street because of their sexuality, or made to feel that they cannot share who they are in a relationship with, or have been bullied because they are straight, or have even been physically attacked because of who they are? And this is not even including the countries where being LGBTQ+ is frowned upon, challenged, or, unbelievably, still illegal.

I love my husband, but the fact is that there are still places where I would not hold his hand or kiss him in public or even tell people that he is my husband. I still get exclamations of surprise from some people when I say that I have a son and that he was adopted with another man (the assumption is that he came from a prior straight relationship). So, even with the privilege that comes from being White, British, and male, I still face prejudice, stigma, and heteronormative assumptions.

I dream of a day when I do not need to say that I am gay, just that I am human, and no one bats an eyelid about my gender or sexuality. But until that day, the letters and labels give us the language of identity we need to describe who we are, a way of finding allies, and allow us to continue campaigning for true societal equality.

Who are you?

Before we get into the meaning of vocabulary and concepts, I would like you to continue to consider why language in this area is so important. The words people use to describe themselves are significant, and even if you do not realise it, probably mean a great deal to you too.

I am going to ask you to start with you. Who are you? The answer to this question will illustrate why this chapter is so important. Everyone has different ways of describing their identity. So, before we continue, I want you to try this: using the template below, write down the words you use to describe who you are around or inside the figure. There is no right answer here, and do not try to write what you think someone else would want to read; use the words you would genuinely use to describe yourself.

Do not overthink it, just put what comes to mind first.

Go!

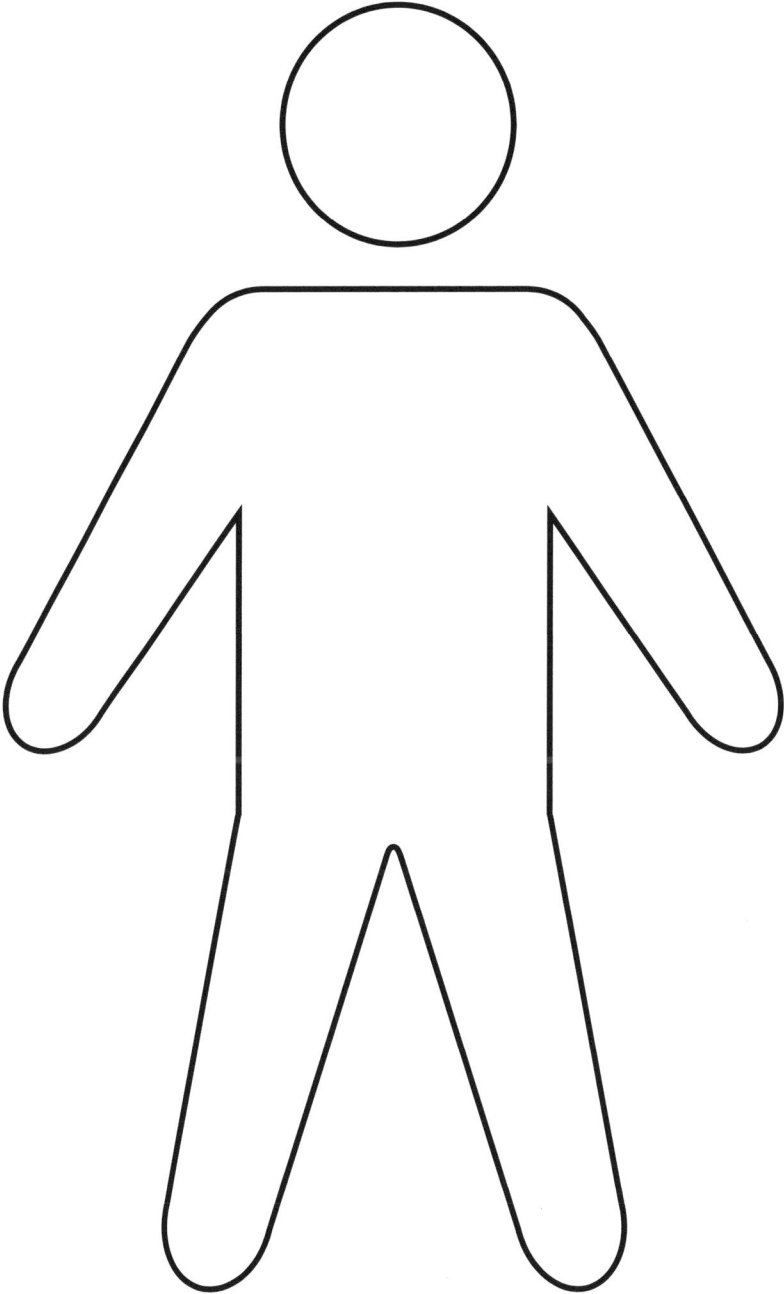

While writing this book, I asked several people to do the same exercise. Here is what they told me about their identity. Take a few moments to look at the similarities and differences between what these individuals wrote about themselves.

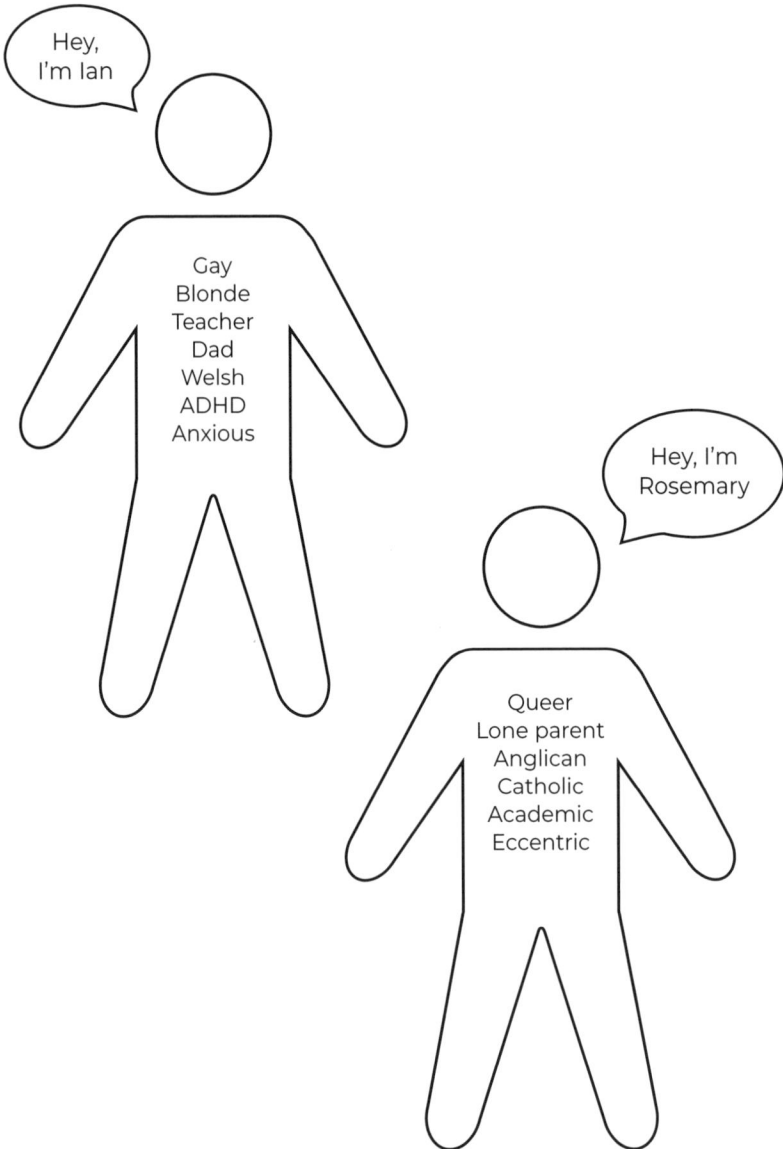

Hey,
I'm Ian

Gay
Blonde
Teacher
Dad
Welsh
ADHD
Anxious

Hey, I'm
Rosemary

Queer
Lone parent
Anglican
Catholic
Academic
Eccentric

Hey, I'm Catrina

Masked
Fearful
Neurodivergent
Burnt out
Anxious
Fruit salad
Bisexual
Authentic

Hey, I'm Ty

Energetic
Challenging
Relentless
Complex
Vulnerable

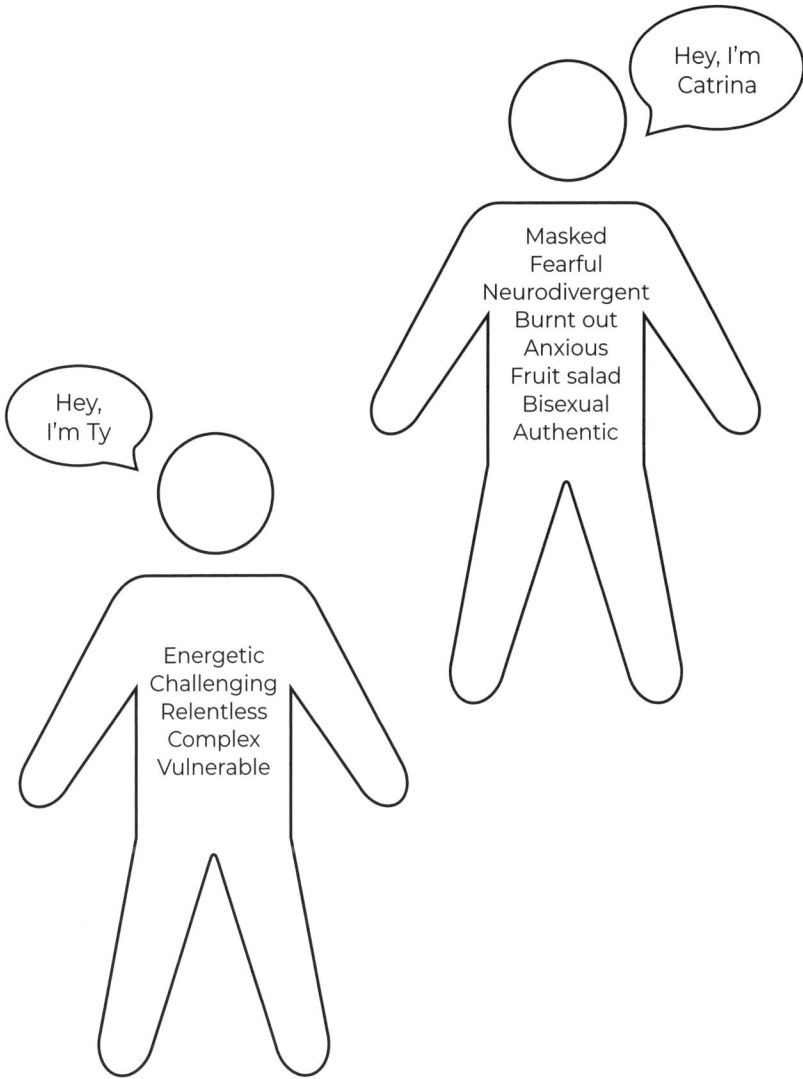

Notice that there are certain attributes present and not present in different people's descriptions. Gay, bisexual, and queer is present, straight is not. Neurodivergent is present, neurotypical is not. Even blonde is present and brown hair is not. If you are straight, perhaps it did not even occur to you to note down your sexuality. If you are a man, maybe it did not cross your mind to record your sex or gender; this is incredibly common and absolutely expected. Very often, the parts of your identity you think about are not the similarities you have with others but the differences. This can be because it has caused challenges in your life or that it makes you feel different to most of the people around you. This is particularly noticeable in Ty's answers, which reveal more about his personality than his identity as most of his characteristics are in line with most of his community. You may have guessed it, but he is a straight, White, neurotypical male.

It can sometimes be difficult to understand why LGBTQ+ people seemingly always want to talk about their sexuality or gender identity. If you are not LGBTQ+, this lack of understanding is simply because you have never had to come out or hide this part of yourself. You have also probably never been in a position where you have had to explain the sex or gender of the person you are in a relationship with or been bullied for that part of your identity. We all have our individual struggles and facets, which is one of the many reasons why society is so interesting; it would be incredibly boring if we all had the same identity and personality. However, when you have to justify your existence or explain why you live the way you do, that part of your identity becomes more prevalent in the way you describe yourself. We also see this commonly when someone may be a minority or a persecuted group in terms of race, disability, religion, or neurodiversity.

Recognising that what we value in our own identity may not be the same as what others value is an important first step in empathising with other people and helps us to look outside our own experiences.

From Ace to Ze: terminology and phrases

If you have ever attended one of my training sessions, you will know that I am never going to stand at the front reeling off the meanings of loads of words (there are far more interesting ways of learning vocabulary). But understanding the most frequently used words and phrases will enable you to hold essential conversations while avoiding misunderstandings and potential conflict around what can be a sensitive topic for many people.

Before we begin exploring some of these themes, there are three words that it is crucial for you and your colleagues to understand: sex, gender, and sexuality.

Sex

Sex refers to the biological differences between males and females. It includes physical attributes like reproductive organs, hormones, and chromosomes that categorise individuals as men or women. Your sex appears on your birth certificate, and in many countries it is a protected characteristic (as discussed in the Introduction). In the UK, this is defined as male or female and relates directly to the role in reproduction.

Gender

Gender refers to the roles, behaviours, and expectations linked to being a man, woman, or non-binary person. It involves how people see themselves and how society sees them, beyond just biological differences. It is a mix of identity, expression, and cultural norms that can differ from person to person and society to society. Think about how someone would describe a man or woman where you live; this will differ in various countries and throughout time, demonstrating that gender is a social construct and not a fixed entity.

Some people are conscious of their gender and may identify it using specific terminology, especially if it does not align with their sex. For example, someone who is male but is non-binary will be more conscious of their gender than someone who is female and lives as a woman. It is likely, though, that you do not think of your gender as a specific part of your identity. This is because it aligns with your sex and so you do not need to consciously think about it. We can talk about this as a 'passive' gender, as you are not con-sciously aware of it.

Sexuality

Sexuality refers to a person's feelings, attractions, and behaviours related to romantic and sexual connections with others and how they express those feelings. In 2022, according to the Office for National Statistics, roughly 93% of the UK population age 16 or over identified as heterosexual or straight and around 3% identified as lesbian, gay, bisexual, or other orientations.[1] This data is inconsistent around the world, mainly because knowing how many people are gay, lesbian, or bisexual relies on them stating it openly, and this can be challenging in some countries.

Now that we have covered the basics, here is your challenge. Give yourself a maximum of two minutes to answer the following questions and then see how you did. Once you have finished, we will explore some of these phrases in more depth, but this start is important so that you get the most from the following chapters.

Once you are done, you can find the answers and explanations on each word at the back of the book. (Feel free to play gameshow music in the background to add to the atmosphere!)

1. Someone who does not have sexual feelings but may still have an active sex life, get married, or have children:
   a. Celibate
   b. Pansexual
   c. Bisexual
   d. Asexual

   ____.

2. Someone who is attracted to men and women:
   a. Homosexual
   b. Heterosexual
   c. Bisexual
   d. Asexual

   ____.

1   Office for National Statistics, Sexual Orientation, UK: 2021 and 2022 (27 September 2023). Available at: https://www.ons.gov.uk/peoplepopulationandcommunity/culturalidentity/sexuality/bulletins/sexualidentityuk/2021and2022.

3. Generally, a word to describe men who are attracted to other men but can also be used by other people who do not identify as homosexual:

   a. Gay

   b. Queer

   c. Bisexual

   d. Pansexual

   _____.

4. Someone whose gender does not match the sex that they were assigned at birth:

   a. Gay

   b. Queer

   c. Pansexual

   d. Transgender

   _____.

5. A woman who is attracted to other women:

   a. Sapphic

   b. Queer

   c. Non-binary

   d. Lesbian

   _____.

6. Someone whose gender is the same as their sex assigned at birth:

   a. Cisgender

   b. Straight

   c. Pansexual

   d. Lesbian

   _____.

7. An umbrella term to be used interchangeably with other LGBT+ vocabulary or as a way for people to describe themselves outside of 'traditional' relationships and genders:

   a. Queer

   b. Gay

   c. Pansexual

   d. Sapphic

   _____.

8. Someone whose physical sex characteristics do not fall into the strict male/female binary:

   a. Transgender

   b. Queer

   c. Pansexual

   d. Intersex

   _____.

9. Someone whose is attracted to individual people, regardless of their sex or gender:

   a. Sapphic

   b. Queer

   c. Pansexual

   d. Intersex

   _____.

10. Another way of describing someone who is intersex:

    a. Differences in sex development

    b. Queer

    c. Pansexual

    d. Transgender

    _____.

11. Someone who does not identify as a man or a woman:

    a. Non-binary

    b. Queer

    c. Pansexual

    d. Intersex

    ___.

Now that you have finished, you can check your answers on page 173 and find out more about each term. It might be useful to sit with this vocabulary for a while and consider whether there were any misconceptions or gaps in your knowledge and, if so, why that might be.

While some of these terms are commonly known, it is likely that most of the population will not get 100% of them correct. In the rest of the chapter, we will explore some of these terms and relate them to your work in schools. It can be useful to recap this vocabulary regularly with staff, as we need to ensure there is a shared understanding.

One important point to note is that people often have different interpretations of some of these words. For example, some individuals would say that trans women (someone assigned male at birth and living as a woman) can be lesbians, while others disagree. Policing language to the extent of telling people who they are is the opposite of inclusion, so during this work it is essential to emphasise that everyone is entitled to their opinion. However, regardless of your viewpoint, this is no excuse for deliberate prejudice.

The queer issue

As a grammarian and word geek, I find the word 'queer' incredibly interesting. Growing up, queer was a pejorative word and often used as an insult or disparaging term. However, much like other minority communities who have been labelled with offensive names, portions of the LGBT+ community have begun to reclaim this term and call themselves and their social groups queer, extending LGBT+ to LGBTQ+ (more on these initialisms and which ones to use will be discussed later in this chapter).

You might be confident using the word 'queer', confused by the different opinions, or wary of using it at all. To really understand the word, we need to know where it comes from, so let us go on a brief historical journey.

Queer is actually a very old word in the English language, with evidence of it in writing from the 16th century.[2] Originally meaning odd or strange, by the 19th century, the word had become a derogatory term for gay men. In fact, evidence presented at the trial of Oscar Wilde described him as a 'snob queer'.[3] Throughout the 20th century, queer was used to degrade gay men, but by the 1960s and 1970s, as the gay and lesbian rights movements were gathering momentum, people started to reclaim the word. (Lots of teenagers love to think that it is their generation that is reclaiming queer, not realising that this discussion has been going on for half a century.) In recent years, the use of queer has had a resurgence, particularly among young people as a way of describing their identity or as a collective term for groups of LGBT+ people.

This complex history of queer goes some way to explaining why there is such debate about the word. It has now evolved and can be thought of in a few ways: as a collective term for the LGBT+ community, as a word to describe people who do not feel that the other available terminology fits their gender or sexual identity, and as a word to be used interchangeably with other LGBT+ terms.

The power of queer is that it means different things to different people, but this is also its downfall, as it can also be used as a term of derision or ridicule. I have no problem with other people using queer to describe themselves (it is not my place to determine someone else's identity), but it is not a word I generally use for myself; I prefer gay. When I was in school, queer was one of the most prominent words used to bully me, but as I have got older, I have become more comfortable hearing it. In fact, in 2025, I launched a clothing range, Bring Queer, to raise money for LGBTQ+ education. (I am quite the contradiction.) So, if even I have a

---

2   Oxford University Press, 'Queer', *OED Online* (2018). Available at: https://www.oed.com/dictionary/queer_n2.

3   M. Goldby, A Note on the Term 'Queer' [blog], *Museum of Croydon* (2023). Available at: https://museumofcroydon.com/blogs-queer-croydon/blog-post-title-two-nl5fj.

complex relationship with queer, and I am writing a book about LGBTQ+ inclusion, do not beat yourself up if you are unsure of the word.

In schools (and, indeed, the wider world), here is my advice:

✚ Only describe someone using queer if you know that they use the word for themselves.

✚ Avoid using the term to describe the whole LGBT+ community but do use it as part of it – for example, LGBTQ+.

✚ If you are not sure how someone feels about it, ask.

✚ Do not be afraid of the word. If the people around you are comfortable with using it, do not make it taboo – that is where its power as an insult lies.

It is crucial that we have conversations like this one with young people. Many do not appreciate the complexity of the word 'queer' and use it without respecting its history and complexity. Young people should feel empowered to use the word in appropriate situations, but they should also understand that not everyone is comfortable with it.

LGB or LGBT or LGBT+ or LGBTQ+ or LGBTQIA+ or 2SLGBTQIA+ or LGBTQQIP2SA+?

I am going to let you in on a secret: there is no one right answer to this question, so you can give yourself a break. People very often overthink which initialism to use, but in the wider conversation around inclusion, it is a small issue. There is no 'official' abbreviation, but to decide which is the right one to use, ask yourself a question: who am I talking about? You might have spotted already that I have used several versions so far in this book. Understanding who we are talking about will clarify why and when the different forms are used.

One of my hobbies is grammar, and so I cannot resist explaining that these are initialisms rather than acronyms, because when you say them, you say each letter individually rather than as a word. You have no idea how happy I am that I managed to get a grammar fact into a book about LGBTQ+ inclusion.

If we are talking about sexuality, it is perfectly acceptable to use the term LGB+, as these are the terms associated with sexuality. If we are talking about marginalised genders and sexualities, we might use either LGBT+ or LGBTQ+; it is simply personal preference. If we are also referencing people who are intersex or asexual, we can expand it to LGBTQIA+. Deciding which term to use is all about who is the focus and ensuring that the initialism reflects them.

You may also notice that '+' appears on all the initialisms I have used. As society has progressed and our understanding of identities has deepened, the need for a more encompassing term became apparent. The addition of the '+' signalled a shift towards inclusivity, acknowledging that the spectrum extends beyond the original categories of gay and lesbian. This change opens up a more welcoming space for those whose identities do not fit neatly into the initial framework, but it also prevents the initialism from becoming an unwieldy term that loses its meaning.

In North America, the term 'two-spirit' evolved in the 1990s. It is often used by Indigenous people as an alternative to transgender or non-binary to reflect the diversity of ways that gender non-conforming people are viewed by their respective communities. Using the two-spirit label outside of these communities is viewed as appropriation, so it would be correct to add '2SL' to the initialism only if you are specifically talking about two-spirit communities. It is not an appropriate term to use about Europeans, for example, as European communities do not have the concept of two-spirit.

Throughout this book, I will be using the initialism LGBTQ+. This is because I am primarily talking about these identities, but it is also becoming the de facto initialism used by many governments and institutions. When I use a different initialism, it indicates that I am discussing a specific group – for example, only LGB+ people.

However, I will conclude by reiterating that you should not worry yourself too much about which initialism you use. As long as you are not excluding out of prejudice, no one is going to shout at you for using a different abbreviation (at least, they should not).

But I did not mean it like that

As we are exploring language, I would like you to consider what makes a word an insult. We have already explored queer and the complexities around this word, so it is not always as straightforward as creating a list of insults and acceptable words.

Understanding whether a word is an insult usually depends on context and intent. The same word can be used in different ways and with different impacts. For example, the term 'gay' can be used neutrally to describe someone's sexual orientation or disparagingly to demean or insult. Context clues, such as the speaker's tone, body language, and setting in which the word is used play a significant role in determining whether a word is intended as a slur.

Intent is also important when identifying insults. If someone uses a word without realising it could be hurtful, it can still cause harm, but it could be argued that, although insulting, the word itself is not an insult. This is not to say that this should be an excuse, but education here is far more important than consequence. It is crucial to help people understand how their words affect others to create a more inclusive environment, but without making them feel they are not allowed to say anything at all.

My favourite T-shirt is a snugly fitting grey one with 'homo' written across the front. The reaction from people when I wear it is fascinating. Some are entertained, some are interested, and some are uncomfortable. Initially, when I saw people's reactions, my first response was to shelve the T-shirt and never wear it again. But as time went on, the rebel and activist in me thought that perhaps this could be my small contribution to reclaiming the term (and I might have loved the attention too). In the past, homo was a commonly used pejorative term, so is it now acceptable? The truth is that it is not entirely accepted. I have used the word jokingly with friends to describe myself and the people I am close to (who I know do not mind the phrase), but, on the whole, it is still seen as an insult. Again, it comes back to context and intent. I am not insulting anyone directly – I am describing myself in an almost comical way – so my intent is positive.

There are many other terms that are similarly controversial and used in different ways by different people. 'Dyke' has been widely reclaimed by the lesbian community. Originally used to describe masculine or 'butch' women, it became a slur for women who are attracted to other women, but it is now used by many women to describe their identity.

Ask someone from Wales or the Midlands what a 'faggot' is, and they will tell you that it is a delicious (or gross, depending on your perspective) meatball made out of minced meat and offal. I am not selling it well, but trust me, with mushy peas, mash, and onion gravy it is the perfect winter food. However, as a pejorative term, it is one of if not *the* most offensive thing you can say to a gay man. Emerging in the 16th century as a term for old women,[4] the evolution of the word is complex, but by the 20th century faggot was being used as a derogatory term for gay men. Although it has not received the same reclaiming as queer, some gay men use it in a jovial or flippant way. But for the majority, if this word is used as an insult, it can evoke fury and hurt. Associated with anti-homosexual agendas during the AIDS crisis, the use of this word should not be taken lightly. Even writing this, the anger I feel towards people who use faggot as an insult is significant. Personally, this is one of the worst metonyms for being gay that could be used to describe me, but thankfully it is not a word that you hear much any more.

There are many other words in this area – such as 'nancy boy', 'poof', 'flamer', 'tranny', and 'fairy' – that are in various stages of being reclaimed or not being used at all. As mentioned earlier, it is essential to consider not only the motivation behind these words, but also the context of the person who is hearing it. It does not matter if the person using the word 'faggot' is comfortable with it if the person hearing it finds it offensive or upsetting. Words have different meanings and values for each of us, but being considerate of other people's feelings is crucial to creating a civil and considerate society.

---

4   Oxford University Press, 'Faggot', *OED Online* (2018). Available at: https://www.oed.com/dictionary/faggot_n.

Transgender identities and gender non-conformity

We have come an incredibly long way in the past decade as to how we talk about identities in schools, with teachers, parents, and pupils all more educated in these areas than ever before. One of the aspects that is the focus of a lot of conversation is how to support pupils who are questioning their gender identity. In Chapters 5–7, we will consider how and when to teach young people about these identities, but first, we will explore some of the concepts and vocabulary surrounding gender identity.

You might never have thought about your gender as different to your sex, and so it may be difficult to relate to someone who has an incongruence between their sex and gender. But understanding how someone in this position feels is not essential; the most important outcome should be that you have empathy with people who are questioning their identity. Even if you do not fully understand what it means to be non-binary or trans, you can still empathise with them as a person. Lack of understanding should never be an excuse for not treating people with kindness and respect.

As gender is socially constructed, it can be perceived in different ways by different people. Some of these ways include the following.

Gender as a social concept

Gender as a social concept refers to the roles, behaviours, activities, and expectations that societies consider appropriate for men, women, and people of other genders. These roles are socially constructed and can differ across cultures and historical periods. Everyone is shaped by these societal norms, even if they do not consciously think about their gender or actively identify with it. This concept can be used to explain, for example, why there are still disparities in pay and job expectations.

Gender as part of identity

For some people, gender is an integral part of their identity – it represents how they perceive and what they know to be true about themselves. This can include terms such as boy, girl, male, female, non-binary, and any of the many gender identities people use to describe themselves. For most individuals, their gender identity aligns with the sex they were assigned at birth, which is typically categorised as male or female. These individuals are referred to as cisgender – for example, a male who identifies as a man. People who see gender as part of their identity may express this via their clothing, names, or pronouns; however, even if it is not visible, it is still an important part of their identity.

Gender as a passive part of identity

Other people may feel that their gender is not a significant part of their identity or may not consciously think about it. I do not consciously think of my gender as separate from my male sex, so I would find it difficult to describe my gender. In this sense, I am gender passive as I do not consider my gender to be a core part of my identity.

Gender non-conformity

Gender non-conformity refers to the expression of gender in ways that do not conform to societal expectations or norms associated with an assigned sex. For instance, stereotypical gender norms suggest that men wear trousers, play with boys' toys, and like masculine colours. In fact, everyone is gender non-confirming in some way as none of us completely adhere to gender stereotypes. Gender non-conformity is not a new concept, and history is filled with examples of people who have challenged societal norms. As with gender identity, many people's gender non-conformity is passive and they do not consciously think about it. Others consider it to be a core part of their identity, and some use it to entirely define their gender alongside other terms such as man, woman, or non-binary.

Someone who describes part of their identity as gender non-conforming may consciously express themselves in a manner that is different from what society traditionally considers masculine or feminine. This expression can manifest itself through clothing, hairstyles, behaviour, or interests that are not aligned with stereotypical gender roles. Schools and parts of society have worked tirelessly to challenge gender stereotypes, so it could be argued that the goal is for everyone to be gender non-conforming and live however they wish. After all, what are girls' and boys' toys?

Although there is an overlap between people who are gender non-conforming and those who are transgender, the first does not necessarily signify the second. Just because someone does not adhere to gender stereotypes, does not mean they are transgender. We need to be careful about labelling children or adults as transgender based on their external appearances or their likes and dislikes.

Transgender identities

Transgender individuals are those whose gender identity differs from the sex they were assigned at birth. For example, someone assigned male at birth who identifies as a woman is a transgender woman. Likewise, someone assigned female at birth who identifies as a man is a transgender man. Being transgender often involves transitioning, which can include social, medical, or legal steps to align their life with their gender identity.

When people transition, we often only see the surface changes, which can include aspects of their identity such as name, pronouns, clothes, and for adults on gender affirming treatments, their physical appearance. This can lead to a misconception that being transgender is just about appearance, but being transgender is far more than that. The feeling that your sex is incongruent with your gender identity is called gender dysphoria, which is a recognised medical condition but is not a mental illness.[5]

Non-binary

For most people, their identity of being a man or a woman is clear to them, but this does not apply to everyone. Non-binary is a collective term for identities that do not fit into the binary of man or woman. Although there are several identities within this group,

---

5 See https://www.nhs.uk/conditions/gender-dysphoria.

most people either consider that they do not identify as a man or woman or may move between them. And just because non-binary people exist, this does not invalidate those who are men or women; it just demonstrates the complexity of human identities.

Those with a non-binary gender still have a biological or legal sex, which is especially important when considering healthcare, which in most countries is recorded on birth certificates and other government documents such as passports. Non-binary people may use the pronouns they/them if they do not identify with he/him or she/her pronouns. They may face challenges when grouped into genders that they do not identify with, so it is essential that we consider everyone when organising groupings and structuring school events and facilities.

Agender

Not to be confused with asexual, which is someone who does not experience sexual attraction, a person who identifies as agender does not identify with any gender. People who are agender often feel they have no gender, or they may feel neutral or indifferent towards gender. This identity is distinct from being a man or a woman, or even non-binary, as it signifies the absence of gender altogether. Agender individuals may use a variety of pronouns, including they/them, or may prefer not to use gendered pronouns at all.

The evolution and devolution of language

The language around sexuality and gender is constantly evolving as our society changes and our understanding of these concepts deepens. The interesting point about the language of gender and transgender identities is the speed with which particular words have been transformed, replaced, or removed from the lexicon entirely. Words such as 'transexual' and 'cross-dresser' have fallen out of use and been replaced with transgender.

One of the problems we are facing currently is people labelling anyone who is gender non-conforming as transgender. For example, a man who dresses using female norms is often categorised as transgender. However, this person may just be gender non-conforming or enjoy wearing women's clothing, and not transgender as they do not have gender dysphoria or an incongruence between their sex and gender identity. In a society as diverse as ours, listening and respecting people's chosen labels is crucial, as only they know how they truly identify.

Recently, we have seen the evolution of 'trans+', which is a more inclusive label and includes a broad range of terms including transgender, non-binary, agender, and anyone who falls outside of the traditional gender binary. This would include people who wear clothing or fashion their appearance to challenge gender norms, but it does not necessarily mean they have gender dysphoria or identify as transgender. Trans+ is a helpful term, but it is worth noting that although it includes transgender, it is not the only identity within it.

As language grows and develops, I would urge you to continue to educate yourself on these new terms, so that we all understand and respect how people describe their own identity.

The situation in schools

Through easy access on the internet and social media, young people are more aware of the language of sexualities and gender identities than ever before. Young people tend to be more confident than adults in using specific labels for themselves, and it is becoming more acceptable for people's labels to change over time. Many are experimenting with their image, names, and pronouns, and challenging the gender binary that has been so prevalent in much of recent history. To maintain the relevance of conversations and the curriculum, all staff in your school need to keep up to date with the vocabulary and terms that are being used, so that you can have discussions with them about their needs.

For the most part, there is little issue with pupils experimenting with their gender identity. In a similar way to sexuality, it can take time for young people to work out exactly who they are. I am 42, and my identity is still growing and developing. However, the shift in societal views towards identities has caused challenges for schools whose processes, policies, and procedures have not kept up with these changes. There is little to no evidence to suggest that there is any long-term harm in allowing pupils to socially explore their gender identity.[6] This is very different, of course, to young people medically transitioning. As educators, we are not clinicians, so we should not be recommending any medical transition treatments, such as binders or hormones; this should be left to medical professionals.

Anecdotally, I have heard from schools where pupils are starting school at age 3 already being labelled as transgender. Many transgender people explain that they were aware they were transgender at this age, so we must not diminish their experiences. However, there are also instances where parents have labelled their child based on stereotypical traits, such as the toys they play with or the clothes they like to wear. This is problematic in several ways. First, it does not acknowledge what being transgender means, reducing it to appearances rather than an internal sense of self. Second, it is based on archaic stereotypes which schools and wider society have been fighting for decades. Third, if pupils are being labelled as transgender, rather than gender non-conforming or trans+, then there is a risk that those children with gender dysphoria who need support are lost in the crowd. Finally, there is the potential for schools to face accusations of grooming or indoctrination. The key issue here is, who is the person deciding that the child is transgender? Where is the voice of the child? It is unlikely that a child this young would be able to articulate gender dysphoria, so this label may be coming from an external source rather than the child.

Schools must strike a careful balance between supporting gender-diverse young people and ensuring that society does not roll backwards on tackling gender stereotypes. Your aim should be to create an inclusive environment where pupils who are gender diverse have the confidence to be themselves, but also demonstrate

---

6   R. Hall, J. Taylor, C. E. Hewitt, C. Heathcote, S. W. Jarvis, T. Langton, and L. Fraser, Impact of Social Transition in Relation to Gender for Children and Adolescents: A Systematic Review, *Archives of Disease in Childhood*, 109 (2024): s12–s18. Available at: https://adc.bmj.com/content/109/Suppl_2/s12.

that sex and gender should not limit what they like or dislike or what they can achieve in life.

Are you allowed to say 'boys' and 'girls' any more?

Yes, you are allowed to refer to children collectively as boys and girls. Perhaps I should leave it at that. However, in recent years, there has been a lot of debate around inclusive language in schools. A prevailing myth is that educators are no longer allowed to address their pupils as boys or girls due to concerns about gender sensitivity. However, this is simply not true. First, I am going to ask you to consider the pantomime. For those in the know, a pantomime is a British pastime of over-the-top theatre, music, and spectacle, often staged at Christmas. Many scripts begin with, 'Ladies and gentlemen, boys and girls ...' I am a firm believer that this is part of the tradition of pantomime, and it would be a shame to get rid of a phrase that fills many people with a sense of joy because of the tradition behind it. However, it is also true that some pupils, particularly those who are non-binary, may not feel that they identify as a lady or gentleman, boy or girl. Therefore, in school, you may wish to consider calling the group by their class name, or as 'children', or as a friend of mine calls his class, 'folks'.

Myths like these often stem from an insistence on a dichotomy where everything is *always or never*, but this is rarely the case. Situations in schools are impacted by a multitude of factors, including the diverse make-up of the community and the history and ethos of the school – let alone the fact that every child is unique. The origin of suggesting that you cannot say boys and girls any more likely originates from advice in three areas: uniform, grouping for activities such as sports, and how to address pupils.

For several decades, schools have been encouraged to remove the requirements for girls to have one uniform and boys another. In my own school in the 1990s, boys in the year above me supported protests by sixth-form girls for a unisex uniform by dressing up in skirts until the policy was changed. Most schools now have options for uniforms (including skirts or trousers), but they are not usually labelled as boys' or girls' uniforms. This gives pupils a choice without restricting them by sex or gender. Just because the uniform is not labelled as for boys and girls does not mean that boys and girls don't exist.

I once watched a lesson where there was a boys vs. girls quiz, and when the boys won, the teacher commented that the boys always won. In a world where we still have a gender pay gap and women are less likely to be promoted than men, this narrative of pitting boys against girls cements the idea that this is a good thing in society. I get asked many questions around whether we should separate boys and girls for sport in schools. In secondary schools, they should be separated because puberty gives male bodies inherent advantages in many competitive sports. However, in primary schools, this advantage is not present for most pupils, so mixed-sex events can make the logistics much easier and create a more inclusive environment.

This is a prime example of an area where people can become very passionate on both sides. No one should feel guilty about referring to children as boys or girls, but where we can make our groupings more inclusive, then we should do so. It is about sensible balance and ensuring that our motivations are sound.

Litter trays and water bowls

Okay, I am going to cover this very briefly and put it to bed right here. If you listen to the conspiracy theorists and some disreputable newspapers, you might believe that our schools are filled with children identifying as animals or even weirder things. I do not think my editor will allow me to swear here, so you will just have to imagine the expletives I have used when people try to tell me that pupils are identifying as 'furries'.

You might not be able to tell, but this makes me so angry that I am typing incredibly hard (sorry keyboard). Let us get this straight: someone pretending they are a cat is not an identity in the same way that being LGBTQ+ is. They do not truly believe they are a cat. Quite frankly, if they do, then that is a mental health issue. What they are doing is cosplay; they are roleplaying. Not only does calling this an identity make a mockery of actual identities, but it is harmful to movements to improve inclusion.

Children will always push boundaries, and many are reading about this rumour on social media and copying it. They are seeing what they can get away with. So, what do we do if a pupil says they identify as a cat? First, we do not want to humiliate them, but we should not feed into it. Second, dressing up as a cat would not adhere to your uniform policy. Third, identifying as an animal is not a protected characteristic. And that is it. We would not allow a child who was obsessed with Wonder Woman to come to school dressed as them every day and disrupt the class with their superhero antics. We would put a stop to it. This is no different.

There is one just exception. Some children with additional learning needs or who are neurodivergent sometimes find comfort in wearing particular items of clothing or making animal noises. These can be acceptable as reasonable adjustments to make them more comfortable. But let us be clear: that does not mean they are identifying as an animal; they are acting as one.

Empathy over understanding

I have given you a lot of information in this chapter, and it may be that you need to take time to process it or come back to certain aspects. People tend to get very hung up on understanding everything in this area, but none of us can truly know what it is like to be someone else.

As a White, cisgender man, I have no idea what it is like to be subjected to racism or sexism, but I can empathise that it is awful. Even if you do not fully understand some of these topics, you can still empathise with those who are finding things tough. Lack of knowledge is no excuse for not supporting others who are struggling or standing by while they are exposed to prejudice, bias, or bullying. I want you to hold on to that notion as we move into exploring how you and your school can move forward with your LGBTQ+ provision. Do not let understanding get in the way of empathy and progress.

Chapter 2

Mirror, Mirror on the Wall, Who is the LGBTQ+est of Them All?

．．

W hat was a 1990s gay? Well, personally I don't remember any representation or conversations about being gay. That doesn't mean there weren't gay men on our screens, but there were so few that the majority of people missed it. When there was representation, it was often stereotypical or negative and was often met with a backlash from some media outlets.

The first romantic kiss between two men in a British television soap opera was in 1989 in *EastEnders*. I was too young to watch this, so I was not aware of the repercussions, including from politicians who claimed that the scene promoted 'perverted practices' and that the future of *EastEnders* should be reconsidered.[1]

My first memory of seeing an LGBTQ+ person was Hayley Cropper in *Coronation Street* in 1998. Although not something that I could relate to personally, it was the first time I'd seen an individual who fell outside of the traditional norms of people and relationships. I find it remarkable to think that the character was met with such affection and love at the time. What a far cry from what we often see today.

But the watershed moment for me came in 1999 when Russell T. Davies' *Queer as Folk* came out on Channel 4. Gays on TV? Outrageous. I *knew* that it was wrong, but I would sneakily wait until my parents had gone to bed and watch an episode, constantly nervous that they would walk in and find out my secret. The programme showed me a whole world that I did not know

---

1   T. Pearce, LGBT representation on TV Through the Ages – from *EastEnders'* First Gay Kiss to Transgender Superheroes, *Metro* (24 June 2020). Available at: https://metro.co.uk/2020/06/24/lgbt-representation-tv-major-moments-12894718.

existed. I cannot understate the impact this had – to realise that there were people who felt like me who were just living their lives. But also, that they weren't all the same. They weren't all the camp sidekick or being bullied for who they were, but complex people with different personalities and varied lives.

But, in a strange way, *Queer as Folk* reinforced to me that being gay was wrong. Because if it wasn't, why was I having to watch it in secret? And why was it portraying these people who were doing things that everyone was telling me were wrong? Certainly, no one ever talked about *Queer as Folk* in school, even though I now know that pretty much all my friends watched it at the time. Even if I couldn't accept that it was okay to be gay at the time, it helped to shape my understanding that there were other gay people in the world, and if they could be happy, then maybe, one day, so could I.

I know that a lot of LGBTQ+ people owe at least part of their journey of self-discovery to Russell T. Davies. In the very unlikely event that RTD is reading this, thank you!

. . . .

One approach to improving LGBTQ+ inclusion in your school might look like the following:

Action plan

+ Buy inclusive books for the library.
+ Set up a Pride club.
+ Pride Month: early years – paint rainbows to go around the school; Years 1 and 2 – draw pictures of different families; Years 3 and 4 – colour in Pride flags; Year 5 – learn about Marsha P. Johnson; Year 6 – learn about Alan Turing.

Fabulous. Or is it?

When an individual or a group in a school realises that things need to change with respect to inclusivity, the first step is often to make quick, visible gestures – putting up flags, decorating the school with rainbows, creating a display – but this alone will not foster genuine inclusion. When part of a wider plan, these events can contribute to the development of an inclusive school, but on their own they are unlikely to have a substantial or long-lasting impact. To create real change, it is not just the resources and events that need to change, it is the culture.

But before I ask you to consider what you are going to do, I want you think about *who* is going to do the work and *how* to ensure that the process reflects a wide range of voices to avoid the risk of groupthink. If you rely on a small, homogenous group to drive this work, you will limit the perspectives and ideas that inform your actions. Groupthink – when everyone in the room is inclined to agree and avoid challenging each other's ideas – can quickly take hold, leading to well-meaning but superficial or misguided efforts. To bring about meaningful change, you need diversity, not just in the actions you take but in the voices shaping those actions. Your school, like the individuals in it, must engage in self-reflection and seek out a broad range of experiences and viewpoints. This is one way to challenge ingrained biases and avoid falling into the trap of simply doing what is easiest or most visible.

When thinking about who should be part of this change-making process, I would ask you to consider whether you have consulted pupils, staff from various roles, parents, and even the wider community. A top-down approach, where decisions are made by a few individuals in leadership, will not capture the rich diversity of perspectives that exist within a school community. Instead, forming a team that includes a range of voices – teachers, support staff, parents, and pupils – will ensure that the actions you take are reflective of the community you are aiming to serve.

It is understandable that schools may start with simpler, more obvious actions – after all, change can feel daunting, so it is easy to begin with what feels most accessible. But to move beyond tokenism, you need to widen the scope of who is involved and ensure that you are not simply doing 'things and stuff' to tick a box but making thoughtful and deliberate efforts to create an inclusive and supportive environment for everyone.

In this chapter, we will explore how to find the right people to identify where you are as a school, how to bring in diverse perspectives, and what you need to consider to avoid groupthink and gain a more accurate picture of your school community.

Will the token gay please stand up?

I am always surprised by how often I see DEIB work falling to an individual (at least initially). It is incredibly common when developing any part of inclusion and diversity that the champion is someone with lived experience. It is unsurprising that this person will be a passionate advocate for change, but that does not mean that they are an expert: just because someone is bisexual, for example, does not mean they understand what an LGBTQ+ inclusive curriculum entails. A person of colour does not automatically know how to tackle racism. A person with a disability does not miraculously know how to ensure that the school is accessible for people with all disabilities.

Aside from unrealistic expectations about their knowledge, this is also a significant amount of responsibility for one person. For years, I consciously (and unconsciously) avoided conversations about tackling homophobic bullying in the schools where I worked because I did not want to revisit my own traumatic experiences. Many people from minority or under-represented groups have been bullied or experienced bias and prejudice, so why should they be the ones to fix things? It is not that individual who needed to change, it was the people around them. These people should be empowered to drive change *if* they wish to be the spearhead, but we should avoid them becoming the token person with all responsibility for change resting on their shoulders.

It is also surprising how often this work falls to new LGBTQ+ members of staff who are young and enthusiastic (but maybe a bit naive) about change. I cannot count the number of times I have spoken to teachers in the first few years of their careers who have completed reviews, written ambitious action plans, and spent hours in meetings with external providers, only to be told that there is no time or budget, or that they can limit their activities to a Pride club or putting up a display – neither of which will achieve any meaningful change in isolation. This is not to say that teachers just starting out cannot be amazing leads in this area, but if the wider team are not in place, then it will be a non-starter. Without a senior leader (preferably the head teacher) on board, it is likely that DEIB work will be limited in its impact.

Regardless of your role in the school, you need to begin this process by building a diverse team who will first find out where you are as a school and then put into place an action plan that will change your school culture to the benefit of all.

Avoiding the echo chamber

A diversity of voices, opinions, and lenses will help you to build a more accurate and honest picture of where you are as a school and lead to changes that reflect the wider school community. Should this process lie on the shoulders of an individual, it is reasonable to assume that not only will this task be overwhelming, but they are also unlikely to have access to the broad range of data points that will provide a comprehensive and bias-free (as far as this is possible) viewpoint. So, when beginning the process of identifying where you are as a school, a small team or group will be able to collect far more data in the same amount of time and will also bring a more varied range of experiences.

When selecting these individuals, you will naturally lean towards allies who share your beliefs, who probably want the same outcomes, and perhaps who are members of the same community. We often see that the people running LGBTQ+ clubs or driving change in this area are LGBTQ+ themselves. While this will make the initial process easier (as you are less likely to need to convince them that change is needed), it risks creating an echo chamber where only certain voices are heard, which will result in a narrow view of the school's current provision. Therefore, it is preferable to also bring on board staff members who may be slightly resistant to the process or do not have lived experience in this area. But how do we encourage these people to get involved, and how do we open up a dialogue with them?

Conversations around sexuality and gender can be profoundly challenging for many individuals for a variety of reasons. One significant factor is our deeply ingrained biases. We all have them without exception. The difference is whether we are aware of or accepting of them. Having unconscious biases is perfectly natural – they are a result of evolution and neurological development – but that does not mean we cannot change, tackle, or mitigate them.

Some people may believe that being gay is unnatural, that bisexuality does not exist, or that young people can be groomed into being transgender. For the most part, these views originate from the media, social media, or conversations that have given them part of the truth or a skewed version of reality. Although it can be challenging to shift the mindset of these individuals, their input is also essential because you need to understand their thoughts, motivations, and values in order to counter them.

Additionally, cultural and religious beliefs often play a significant role in influencing how individuals perceive sexuality and gender identity. Fear of rejection, discrimination, or misunderstanding from family, friends, or society at large can hinder open dialogue. Furthermore, the lack of comprehensive education and awareness about diverse sexual orientations and gender identities contributes to the difficulty in navigating these conversations. All these factors combined create a complex landscape where individuals may feel hesitant or even unsafe when engaging in discussions about sexuality and gender, which highlights the importance of fostering understanding, acceptance, and inclusivity in these conversations.

People who are resistant to DEIB work may not be intimately involved in your analysis of the school community or in its implementation, but I would urge you to hear their voices, listen to their concerns, and take an approach that does not ignore their lived experience.

Building a team

Approaching people who may be opposed to this work starts with empathy and understanding. Not everyone will be as comfortable or enthusiastic about LGBTQ+ inclusion as you might be, but that is exactly why their input is valuable. Resistance often stems from unfamiliarity, fear of saying the wrong thing, or deeply ingrained biases. Try to approach these conversations with an open mind and be ready to listen as much as to persuade.

Start by framing the issue in a way that highlights shared goals: a better school environment, a sense of belonging for all pupils, and a school community that reflects the values of respect and care.

The conversation should not be framed as 'us' versus 'them' but rather as a collective effort to improve the school for everyone. If people do not understand the purpose of this work, they simply will not become invested.

For instance, instead of focusing solely on LGBTQ+ inclusion, you could approach a colleague by saying something like: 'We're trying to figure out how to make our school a more welcoming place for everyone. I think your input could really make a difference in that conversation. Would you be up for helping us think about how we can make that happen?'

This phrasing opens up the conversation in a non-confrontational way, emphasising collaboration and the idea that their input is not only welcome but necessary. Who would not want to make the school more welcoming for everyone?

For those who may have reservations, listen to their concerns without immediately pushing back. People may worry that they lack the knowledge or experience to contribute meaningfully, or they might feel that LGBTQ+ inclusion is not aligned with their own beliefs. In these cases, reassure them that the process is about learning and growing together, not about having all the answers from the start.

For example, you might say: 'I understand that this might feel new or outside your comfort zone, but that's exactly why your involvement could be really helpful. This process is about learning together, and we could all benefit from your perspective.'

If someone expresses concerns based on personal or cultural beliefs, try to respond with sensitivity. Acknowledge their views but reinforce the school's commitment to creating an inclusive environment for all pupils. The goal is not to change their personal beliefs but to find common ground in ensuring that every child feels safe and supported in school.

For those who might be hesitant, creating small, manageable entry points may help to ease them into the process. Rather than asking someone to take on a large role right away, invite them to participate in a discussion, observe a meeting, or offer feedback on a draft plan. The goal is to build their confidence and allow them to contribute in a way that feels comfortable at first. Over time, as they become more familiar with the work, they may become more engaged.

Additionally, acknowledge that this process can be uncomfortable for many people, especially when addressing personal biases or long-held views. Make it clear that the environment you are fostering is one of learning, reflection, and growth. Mistakes will happen, but they are part of the process. A school community that allows space for people to admit what they do not know, ask questions, and grow in their understanding will be more effective in achieving lasting change.

It can also be helpful to approach people who may not have directly expressed an interest in LGBTQ+ issues but have shown a commitment to pupil well-being, inclusion, or safeguarding in other areas. Often, those individuals who care deeply about pupil welfare can be great allies in this work, even if they have not previously engaged with LGBTQ+ topics. By emphasising the overlap between LGBTQ+ inclusion and their existing priorities, you can find common ground and encourage them to get involved. For example: 'You've done such great work around improving mental health support in our school. I think there are real connections between that work and the work we're trying to do on LGBTQ+ inclusion. Do you think we could explore how those two areas might come together?'

When asking people to be part of the team driving LGBTQ+ inclusion, it is not just about getting volunteers, it is about building a coalition of diverse perspectives. By addressing people's concerns with empathy, framing the issue in terms of shared goals, and creating space for growth and learning, you will build a more inclusive and committed group. Importantly, by engaging those who may resist initially, you ensure that the school's approach reflects the true diversity of its community and avoids the pitfalls of groupthink.

Won't somebody please think of the children?

Very often, there is one voice missing from this process: the pupils. Judy Halbert and Linda Kaser, as part of their Spiral of Inquiry framework, refer to this stage as 'scanning' and suggest that:

All too often it is adults who decide what is right or wrong with learners – and what is good for them – without involving pupils themselves in either identifying issues or developing solutions. Deciding what is going on for learners without their input lacks respect and is less likely to lead to productive change.[2]

This is especially important with issues where the pupils are closer to the changes than the adults. It is essential that as educators we use our professional judgement to interpret their views, but to ignore their voices completely defeats the point of making sure that this is a curriculum and school *for* your learners. You may decide to create a formal pupil group who feed into diversity and inclusion efforts, or to be more flexible by having informal conversations, or use tools such as surveys to gather their views. There is no right answer: you must do what you think is right for your pupils and your community and use a method that will gather the most insightful information.

Secondary age pupils tend to be honest to the point of brutal and, in my experience, will give you a very realistic picture of what is going on in the school. Whether you are creating a pupil group or having informal conversations, it is important to include a cross-section of children and young people, so that you know you are capturing a range of diverse perspectives. It is also beneficial to speak to LGBTQ+ pupils directly. This can give you information on how inclusive the sex education is and what their experiences as LGBTQ+ pupils are. Of course, please do this with caution. You do not want to 'out' any pupils; they should be given a safe space to

2   J. Halbert and L. Kaser, *Leading Through Spirals of Inquiry: For Equity and Quality* (Winnipeg: Portage & Main Press, 2017), p. 31.

talk away from other pupils in front of whom they may not want to open up.

In primary school, this work is more challenging as you do not necessarily want to engage pupils in conversations about these topics before they are ready. At the very earliest, I would talk to Year 6 pupils, but only about bullying, representation, and their experiences of gay as a pejorative word. Other data collection methods, such as teachers auditing the curriculum, are going to be more valuable.

The Avengers

You cannot create a truly inclusive school on your own, and you should not have to. If I have learned anything from Marvel films and comics, building a team is the first and most critical step towards meaningful, lasting change.

Approach this process with intention. Talk to your colleagues, listen to their concerns, and show them how they can contribute. Frame this as a collective effort to create a better school for everyone – a school where every pupil, staff member, and parent feels safe, valued, and respected.

As we have seen, it is not just about including the obvious allies or the most vocal advocates. You need a diverse group that brings varied perspectives, including those who may challenge or question this work. Their input will make your efforts stronger, more thoughtful, and, ultimately, more effective.

Think about your pupils too. How can their voices help to guide you? Whether it is through formal groups, surveys, or informal conversations, find ways to include them in shaping the changes you are making.

Also, consider how many times you have walked past a display that is tattered and out of date, but no one has done anything about it because it has been there for so long. You do not always see what is in front of you, particularly in our own school, so you may want to consider getting in an external consultant to help you answer your DEIB questions and develop an understanding of where you are (insert shameless plug for my services here – please feel free to get in touch for help!). This comes with cost implications, of course, but it can often work out to be more cost-effective in the long run, as they can help you to approach change in an efficient way, and they will see things that you will not.

No matter who you eventually decide to involve in this part of the process, having a range of perspectives will give you the information you need to answer the questions in the next chapter and make a plan that will truly make every child feel safe, seen, and supported. Together, you can take the first steps in creating a school community where every child feels like they truly belong.

Avengers assemble!

Chapter 3

Queer Eye for the School Guy

. . . .

I was 16, and despite hiding the bullying I'd received, I'd held it together. I got good GCSE grades and breezed into the A levels that I wanted to do in sixth form (not bragging – okay, maybe a little bit). Quite a few of the bullies who had made my school life hell had left school after their GCSEs. Then something weird happened: I became popular.

Until this point, being academic was not rewarded in school because all that mattered was how well the boys' rugby team did. Suddenly, it became about how many pupils got into Oxbridge and what your A level results were predicted to be. In friendship groups, intelligence and being academic were now valued, and the class clowns were looked down on rather than being lauded. It was a very odd feeling. I had also started to grow into my looks and people were actually calling me good looking. It was all going Ian's way.

But it wasn't the fairy-tale ending to school it should have been. Whether it was because of the raging hormones, the vacuum created by several of my bullies leaving school, or the unresolved issues surrounding my sexuality, or a combination of them all, things started to fall apart. After starting sixth form well, I began to smoke heavily, drink to excess, and take drugs. My double life continued, although it was now divided into three: the academic teacher's pet, the geek at home who fancied boys, and the teenager pushing every boundary and engaging in riskier and riskier behaviour.

No one outside of my immediate circle had any idea that the other circles existed. In school, I appeared to be the conscientious pupil that I always had been, but inside I was breaking. It was so difficult keeping these personas apart, and I was constantly afraid of letting everyone down if they got a peek into these other lives.

Due to the impact of Section 28, my teachers knew they couldn't talk to me about what was going on (everyone seemed to know that I was gay at this point, apart from me). One teacher knew something was wrong, and although they gave me a safe place during breaks and lunches, the policies, procedures, and provision provided by the school meant that the bullying wasn't dealt with and my mental health wasn't supported.

Miraculously, I managed to get through my A levels and went to study neuroscience at Cardiff University, with a view to becoming a medical researcher or eventually a doctor (which, as you can guess, wasn't very successful).

This was a time to change who I was, to reinvent myself, to finally live authentically as me. But that meant accepting myself for who I was, and for now, that was beyond my grasp.

. . . .

If only this stage of the process was as glamorous as *Queer Eye*: a group of fabulous gay and queer people strut into your school and turn it around in a day. But (and bear with me here), although this process might not have the glitz and glamour of the Fab Five, it will be incredibly empowering and, if you get this right, tremendously rewarding.

In this chapter, we will explore the areas of school life that you will need to evaluate to ascertain exactly how inclusive your school is. As we saw in Chapter 2, this is far more effective when you deploy a team rather than just an individual – and the more diverse these voices are, the better (keep thinking of the Avengers).

I will take you through four threads of inclusion and ask you to consider what the strengths are in your school, but also where you might need to rethink your approaches. (We will examine these threads in more detail in later chapters.) The areas are:

1. Staff knowledge, values, and attitudes.

2. Policies, pastoral, and provision.

3. Representation and role models.

4. Working with the community.

Most importantly in this chapter, I want you to slow down. Think of it like a learning journey in teaching. You, other staff, and the whole school are going to need to learn, unlearn, and process information and skills, knowledge, and attitudes. Only if we do this carefully will it succeed, and you will create a school that is inclusive for all.

What are we looking for?

You have your team in place, you know you want to find out where you are, you might know what areas you need to improve or develop, and you are aware that you do not know what you do not know. But where do you start, especially if you want to avoid identifying only surface-level and virtue-signalling signs of inclusion?

An interesting feature of some schools that are truly LGBTQ+ inclusive is that you may not necessarily see it on a walk around the building. It can be lovely to see Pride flags and lanyards as a visual message of support and allyship, but if this is where it ends, the school is not inclusive. In a school where inclusivity is truly embedded, the signs do not come from rainbow or flag displays but from the people in the building. They come from the way the pupils are confident talking about identities, the representation present in the curriculum, the support networks that form around learners who need them, and the common language and mission of inclusion that unites everyone. This cannot be achieved in a few staff meetings or an INSET day; it requires a long-term approach that may require you and your school to challenge your thinking, biases, and beliefs, and both learn and unlearn.

In many audits, the focus is on areas of interest or activities, such as learning walks, book scrutiny, or lesson observations. While this makes the activity simpler to organise, it presents you with a problem: inclusion cannot be captured entirely in one medium. Let us take representation, for example, which occurs through images on screens, corridor and classroom displays, worksheets, books, and so on. If you assess each of those aspects individually, you will get a fractured view of inclusion that will be challenging to unpick. So, rather than beginning with *where* you will look, the first consideration should be *what* your lines of enquiry will be. These threads can then be explored in various places, giving you a more holistic and realistic picture of your school.

Using the tables on the next few pages, take your time to consider the questions and the areas where you could find evidence. Think about where you might find positive practice, where you might find a lack or poor practice, or areas where you are simply not sure what you are looking for. This exercise is not designed to be a tick list of yes or no questions, but a starting point for you to think about what your priorities should be. Depending on the size of your school, this could be completed as a whole staff or in departments, enabling you to gain the perspective of many stakeholders.

Take your time to work through the questions and note down where there are gaps in your knowledge. Knowing what you do not know is as important as knowing what you do know.

Staff knowledge, values, and attitudes

Let us start with the basics. Do staff have a common understanding of language and concepts, and how do they feel about LGBTQ+ and wider inclusion? From social media to staffroom conversations, there are many misconceptions surrounding all areas of diversity and inclusion, which can lead to misunderstandings or outright prejudice. Gaining a common understanding of these areas and developing a culture of it being okay to say, 'I don't know,' will be key to your success in creating a school where every pupil is safe, seen, and supported.

LGBTQ+ concepts and vocabulary

The sad thing about having information at our fingertips is that it has created a culture where there is a stigma about not knowing what certain terms mean. We need to get rid of this intolerance and create a culture where it is okay to ask what a word or concept means.

Before embarking on training, you may want to ascertain a baseline for staff understanding on LGBTQ+ vocabulary; it may surprise you what gaps there are. One of the best ways is to create an anonymous survey. This anonymity will allow people to be honest and remove the fear of recrimination or embarrassment. While you do not want to quiz staff on their knowledge, you can devise questions focusing on how comfortable they are with the terminology and/or their confidence in this area.

In the Useful Resources section at the back of the book, you will find some example surveys that you can use with staff, parents and carers, and pupils.

For secondary schools, one of the most reliable sources of information can come from speaking to the pupils themselves. Many older pupils, particularly those in sixth form, will have a good understanding of LGBTQ+ vocabulary, and in most schools they will be open in sharing how well (if at all) staff use and understand inclusive terminology. If pupils are not willing to share this information, this gives you an important insight into their openness about LGBTQ+ topics in school.

Ultimately, there is likely to be a huge disparity between different members of staff in their knowledge and confidence, so you will probably have to start at the beginning to ensure consistency and confidence. However, this exercise can give you a good indicator of staff confidence and their feelings around the vocabulary and topics.

Sex and gender

As we saw in Chapter 1, sex and gender are different and there are different attitudes to both. At a basic level, staff should know the definition for each term, but to ensure that the curriculum is fair and balanced, they should also be aware of the sometimes difficult conversations that can arise due to the nature of gender. We need to be careful in how we approach this matter as discussions can become very heated very quickly (you only need to look at social media to see the polarised views on display).

As discussed previously, conducting surveys or interviews can provide insights into teachers' understanding of sex and gender concepts, their comfort level in discussing these topics, and their awareness of gender stereotypes.

LGBTQ+ concepts and vocabulary enquiry questions
How confident are staff with LGBTQ+ concepts and vocabulary?
How well do staff understand the difference between sex and gender?
How confident are staff in supporting a pupil who comes out?
How confident are staff in supporting a pupil who transitions?
How much training on LGBTQ+ inclusion have governors and administrative staff received?

Sources of evidence:

+ Learner and staff voice.
+ Shared drives.
+ Surveys and questionnaires.

Policies, pastoral, and provision

I go to many schools who send me their policies in advance of my visit, often very proud of how inclusive they are. But can I let you in on a little secret? I do not look for the evidence in the policies. Instead, I talk to members of staff and ask them about the policies and procedures. Even if every policy is comprehensive and up to date, if no one knows about them, they do not make a difference. So, when you carry out this part of your health check, make sure you cross-reference what is written down with what people say.

This is also a good opportunity for you to look for ways to slim down your policies. We do not need replication, and we certainly do not need reams and reams of useless information.

One of the best ways to find out whether your policies and provision are effective is to pose certain scenarios to staff members. What would they do if a pupil came out to them? What would they do if the pupil did not want their parents to know? Where would they go for help if a child were struggling with their identity? When do they think you should introduce specific LGBTQ+ vocabulary? All this information should be in your policies, but it is no use if staff do not know where to find it.

I am often asked whether schools need a specific LGBTQ+ policy. In my opinion, the answer is no. If you have an LGBTQ+ policy, do you also have one for race, for religion, and so on? If you do not have a policy for each protected characteristic, I would ask why one aspect of diversity is more important than the others. Now, you may give me a clear reason for this, and if it is necessary for your school and you can justify it, then great. But for most schools, the procedures for supporting LGBTQ+ pupils should appear in other policies where they are most relevant.

Policy enquiry questions
How do the school's policies explicitly address bullying, particularly in relation to protected characteristics such as race, gender, sexuality, or disability?
How are homophobic, transphobic, sexist, ableist, racist, and other prejudiced incidents recorded? Is this consistent with all types of incident?
What mechanisms are in place to ensure that anti-bullying and inclusion policies are regularly reviewed and updated to reflect current issues and best practices?
How are parents and carers involved in understanding and supporting the school's policies on bullying and diversity?

Pastoral and provision enquiry questions
How does the school currently address incidents of bullying, particularly those related to diversity, such as homophobic, racist, or ableist behaviours?

Pastoral and provision enquiry questions
How widespread is the use of the word 'gay' or other slurs in conversational language? Is this recorded accurately in school safeguarding records?
How consistent is the staff approach to tackling bullying incidents?
What specific training or resources are provided to staff to help them support pupils from diverse backgrounds and identities effectively?
How are pupils who are struggling with their identity or want to come out supported by the school and by their peers?
How do parents and staff know what your procedures are when a pupil decides to transition or use non-binary pronouns?
How do you identify and respond to pupils who may need additional pastoral support, particularly those experiencing exclusion or marginalisation?

Sources of evidence:

+ Learner and staff voice.
+ Shared drives.
+ Website and prospectus.
+ Safeguarding software.
+ Governing body reports.

There is potentially a lot of information for you to find in this section. However, before you begin to devise the content of the training that staff are going to receive, you need to ensure that they are supported and protected by your school's policies and procedures. This important detail will prevent teachers, out of goodwill, making mistakes and putting pupils, themselves, or the school at risk.

There is more information on what should be in each policy in Chapter 4.

Representation and role models

It cannot be understated how readily representation and role models are glossed over. The diversity of your health check team is important because we all see the school and curriculum through different lenses. However, it is here that I would ask you to really broaden your lens from LGBTQ+ inclusion to look at all aspects of diversity, so that each pupil feels seen in your school.

When you come to consider disability role models, make sure you look for visible and non-visible disabilities. Where are your role models for attention deficit hyperactivity disorder (ADHD), autism, those with hearing loss, and so on. Also consider your individual setting: are there pupils with particular disabilities or needs who do not see themselves in your school?

This is the part of the process when some people might roll their eyes and claim that we are forcing diversity into the curriculum. And, in a way, they are right. It is not about ticking a list so that every topic is so jammed full of diverse role models that it no longer makes sense. But it is about making sure that our topics and the wider school represent the world we actually live in.

You also need to consider how the organisation of the curriculum changes as the children get older. In the early years, you might read 20-plus picture books on each theme or topic, so it is far easier to include a wide range of representation during each term. But as the children progress through school, they will read longer texts and so fewer books each term – maybe just one core novel. This means that instead of evaluating one topic at a time, you will need to map what representation looks like across multiple topics and year groups. If you survey each topic or year group in isolation, you may not notice whether you lean towards certain characteristics over others. Only by evaluating the phases across the whole school will you gain a true picture of how representative your curriculum is.

Representation and role models enquiry questions
How do you ensure that every pupil is represented in the books they read?
How do your staff ensure that stereotypes are being challenged rather than reinforced in the books that pupils read and the images they see?
Across the curriculum, who are your role models? Where do they come from? What are their characteristics?
What express teaching is there to challenge stereotypes?
What are pupil and staff attitudes to seeing LGBTQ+ symbols and flags around the school?
What is the gender balance in different subjects, and how does this reflect the role models and representation in these areas?

Sources of evidence:

+ Exercise books.
+ Novels and picture books.
+ Classroom and corridor displays.
+ Worksheets and booklets.
+ Website and prospectus.

Working with the community

When you are reflecting on how your community is involved in inclusion, you need to think more broadly than simply parents. Consider with these questions how to involve pupils, all staff (including administrative staff), parents/carers, governors, and important people in the local area, such as religious leaders.

Community enquiry questions
How do you know how your community feels about different areas of diversity, equity, inclusion, and belonging?
How is the community involved in the planning and delivery of a diverse curriculum?
How do community events promote the diversity and cohesion of different communities?
Where are secondary pupils able to go to find allies and people in their own community?
How are inclusion principles, activities, and resources communicated with the community?
How does the community perceive pupils choosing to study subjects that are traditionally associated with a different gender?

Sources of evidence:

+ Policies.
+ Pupil voice.
+ Community voice.
+ Prospectus.
+ Social media.
+ Website.

Time for a cuppa

Answering those enquiry questions may have been challenging for you or your team, or maybe you whizzed through them. There is no correct way. However, I would ask you to reflect on whether you were completely honest, especially around what you do not know. Take some time (and a cuppa) to really sit with what you found out to ensure that you are seeing what is actually there and not what you or your senior leaders want to see.

Everyone has their biases, and there is always a risk that in a desire to avoid shame, we are not truthful with ourselves. Confirmation bias can result in us avoiding the things we need to tackle and instead going for the easy wins in areas where we are not doing too badly.

Impact vs. effort

I am not going to hold back here: discovering the impact/effort matrix was a lightbulb moment for me. Reflecting on my early leadership, I now realise just how many 'school improvement' activities were a complete waste of time and how my energies were often directed to the wrong projects. This meant that many of the mistakes I made during my formative years of subject leadership were filled with incomplete or unsuccessful projects.

Over time, I became better at leadership and led a school from potential special measures to having case studies written about our leadership and curriculum. Without realising it, I was doing the impact/effort matrix in my head.

The impact/effort matrix is a strategic tool used for prioritising tasks or projects based on their potential impact and the effort required to complete them. It is a modern adaptation of frameworks like the Eisenhower matrix, which categorises tasks by urgency and importance, and the Pareto principle, which focuses on the 20% of tasks that yield 80% of results.[1]

The impact/effort matrix refines these concepts by categorising tasks into four quadrants – high impact/low effort, high impact/high effort, low impact/low effort, and low impact/high effort – allowing individuals and teams to focus their resources on tasks that offer the greatest return for the least effort. It has become widely used in business and project management to help streamline decision-making, but it is also useful in schools where time and money are often scarce.

---

1   See D. Buchanan and A. Huczynski, *Organizational Behaviour: An Introductory Text*, 9th edn (Harlow: Pearson, 2019).

The following matrix is an adaptation of the original concept for schools.

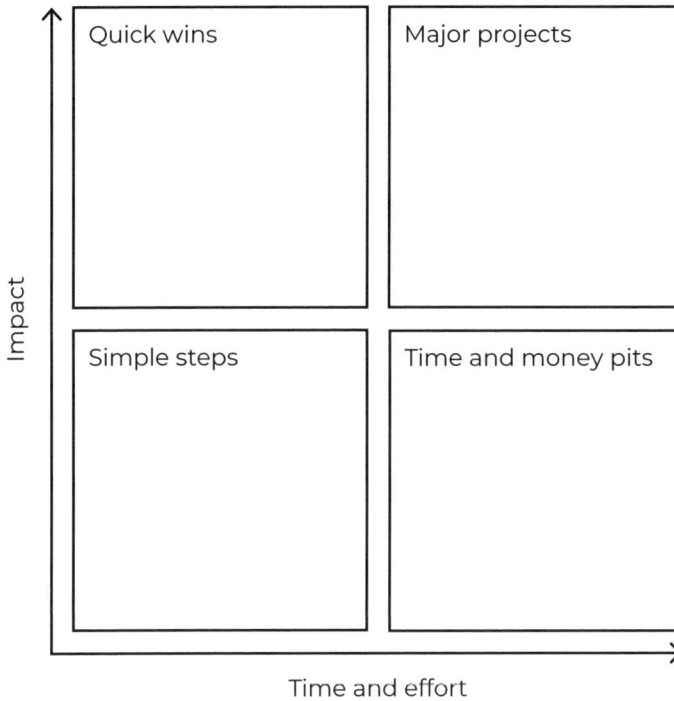

Quick wins	Major projects
Simple steps	Time and money pits

Impact →

Time and effort

Here are some tasks that are commonly used to improve diversity and inclusion in schools:

✚ Put up rainbow flags. (I bet you didn't see that one coming.)

✚ Perform an audit of the curriculum to identify what diverse role models are being taught.

✚ Redevelop the curriculum from the ground up to ensure that it is decolonised and represents the 21st century.

✚ Set up an LGBTQ+ club.

✚ Provide rainbow lanyards for all staff.

✚ Deliver staff training on the importance of inclusive practices.

Have a go at putting these tasks in the matrix for your school. Some will depend on your environment, but others will be consistent for all schools. For instance, redeveloping the curriculum is a huge undertaking but can have incredible benefits, so this would go into the 'major projects' quadrant. Putting up rainbow flags is very low effort but has a low impact in the grand scheme of things, so it would go into the 'simple steps' quadrant.

When schools do not know where to start with inclusion, or where there is a lone voice calling for change, they often fall into the trap of taking only simple steps. On their own, these token gestures are unlikely to create any real change and can actually be damaging in the long term as they tend to be very visible and therefore give the impression that the school is more inclusive than it is. I have been to some schools which look as if a unicorn has exploded and covered the place with rainbows, but in fact it is an unsafe place for many LGBTQ+ young people. I have also been to schools where there is an occasional rainbow lanyard or rainbow flag, but the pupils feel confident to be out and are supported by the school. We need to be mindful and not assume that a school is inclusive merely through the presence of symbols.

Now, I am not suggesting that we should not display rainbows or wear rainbow lanyards. These can be powerful symbols of support and indicate to LGBTQ+ young people who they can talk to about their identity. When I work in schools, it is noticeable how LGBTQ+ pupils are visibly more relaxed around me when I wear a rainbow pin or lanyard. So, if you are confident enough to display a symbol of allyship, please do. But make sure that your inclusion is about more than flags and rainbows.

In the next few chapters, we will explore some suggestions for what you can do to develop inclusion in different areas of your school. As you go through them, it can be helpful to add actions to an impact/effort matrix. This can give you an immediate indication of where your actions should be focused. Ideally, the majority will be in the quick-wins quadrant, with at least one large-scale project in major projects, but it is fine for some to be in the other sections.

Chapter 4
Strong Foundations

• •

I loved university but probably for all the wrong reasons. The bad habits I had developed in sixth form continued and without the restraints of my family home became more entrenched. There was rarely a night when I wasn't drunk or taking one of a cocktail of drugs.

I made some amazing friends in my first year, but I never took the step to be honest with them about who I was. In order to cover up how I really felt, I became a habitual liar. I had a girlfriend for a short time, but it just wasn't right. After we split up, I continually lied about the 'conquests' I'd had and how popular I was with women, despite me rarely getting past second base. My friendships started to crumble around me, because how can you trust someone if you get the sense that they're never being completely honest with you?

In my second year of university, I moved into a student house. With my main priority being to get as drunk as possible each night, I began to disengage from my friends. This was compounded by the hell-hole of a house we lived in, and one by one they moved out. Before I knew it, I was almost alone. But I felt like I deserved it. After all, I was a broken person, so I deserved to be alone.

It was around this time that I met an openly gay man for the first time. From what I remember, he was very attractive and came on to me. I don't remember much else about him, but inside I was tearing in two. Half of me was repulsed by the thought of being with another man, and the other half wanted nothing more than to be with him.

In secret, I completely freaked out. The sense of being wrong, of being broken, of needing to be fixed came rushing back. But I felt like I was damaged and beyond fixing. All those words the bullies had used towards me were true. I was disgusting and bad and should not be allowed to carry on.

I sat alone in my student house and ordered my standard dinner – curry sauce, rice and chips, and a bottle of whisky. I remember sitting on the floor listening to music and the dark thoughts inside me getting louder and louder, so I couldn't shut them out any more.

I don't remember much about what happened next, but I did something to try and end it all. I remember panicking that I had made a mistake. And I remember calling the ambulance before it was too late.

All the bullying and hiding had finally taken its toll, and I couldn't go on any more. I had tried to take my own life. After being rescued just in time, I was taken into hospital and treated. Shortly afterwards, I was released into the care of someone who has kept this secret for almost 20 years.

I only started talking about this episode a few years ago because I was ashamed – not ashamed of what I did but ashamed that I had failed. I couldn't even get that right. I can't pinpoint exactly what it was on that day that tipped me over the edge, but isn't that often the case? If we only ever look for that large trigger moment, and don't stop to look at the wider picture, then we are often missing what is right in front of us.

The leaders of the school I went to as a pupil never did find out what happened to me, and I have since discovered that others in my school went through similar experiences. If only they had known, maybe they would have considered how their school could have been run more inclusively. There are far too many people who have gone through similar experiences. One of the reasons I am writing this book and doing the work I do is because I want to make sure that no one ever goes through what I experienced.

. . . .

So far, we have explored how you can ascertain where you are as a school. In the following chapters, I will be covering various areas of inclusion and taking you through the process of how to make your school more inclusive.

Before diving into these changes, you need to focus on the groundwork. In this chapter, I will help you to create a clear vision for change and think about the policies that underpin your school's approach to inclusion. In order to know what to do, in what order, and how to go about it, we must have an ideal vision of what the future will look like. This takes preparation; jumping in too quickly will result in missed goals and ineffectual changes.

By building a strong foundation, you will ensure that the changes you implement are meaningful, achievable, and supported by the whole school community. This foundation will set the stage for the practical steps ahead, making it easier to create a school where every child feels safe, seen, and supported. With these elements in place, the practical steps in the following chapters will be much easier to implement and will be far more likely to succeed.

Creating a vision statement

Knowing your purpose is crucial if you want to ensure that your school avoids virtue signalling. The most fundamental question we need to ask ourselves is: why are we enacting this change?

When you are creating an action plan, it can be helpful to first develop a statement of inclusion. You may already have a state-ment reflecting your commitment to diversity and inclusion in your school aims, but if you are starting a dedicated DEIB project, it can be beneficial to either revisit the statement or even develop a new or additional aim. Here are some fictitious examples:

+ At Sunnydale Primary School, we celebrate diversity and promote inclusion, ensuring every pupil feels valued and respected. Our mission is to foster a supportive environment where differences are embraced, and all pupils can thrive.

+ RTD Middle School is committed to creating an inclusive community that embraces diversity and promotes equity. We will create a provision where every pupil and family have the education they need to be part of our school community.

+ Callum Scott Howells High School is dedicated to fostering an inclusive and diverse community where all pupils are respected and valued. Our mission is to challenge prejudice and discrimination, promote understanding and empathy, and ensure that every pupil feels empowered to thrive in an equitable environment.

You can see here that, although there are common themes, they all reflect the unique priorities of each school. You can go about this process in several ways, but the core principle must be that your aims are devised by a wide selection of staff. We want this change to be done *with* the staff, not *to* them.

I am going to take you through how I created the vision statement for our school and then discuss some alternative methods.

My school invited a selection of pupils, parents, catering and administrative staff, and governors to a twilight workshop with all the teaching and support staff. Using a seating plan (which was great rehearsal for my wedding), I made sure that every table included a mixture of voices. The aim was to cultivate an environment so that every table heard different viewpoints and opinions. After an introduction, the groups were given one of the following prompt questions:

✢ What does diversity mean for us?

✢ How can embracing diversity help our pupils?

✢ What are our strengths?

✢ What do we need to learn about diversity?

✢ What are our worries about diversity?

In turn, the participants discussed how these questions related to diversity and what they meant for our school. They compiled their thoughts by writing on or attaching sticky notes to an A1 sheet of paper. The sheets were then moved around the room, where the other tables amended, added, or removed comments. This required a lot of trust among the stakeholders, and maybe your school is not there yet, but it worked for us. Once we had collected all the evidence, the senior leadership team (SLT) distilled the points raised into a statement of diversity. The workshop also gave us significant information about what our stakeholders thought about the journey, which let us plan accordingly.

A second option is to gather this information through a survey or questionnaire. If you allow participants to be anonymous, people may be more honest, but you will not know who has answered and so will not know whether you have got a representative sample of your school population. This method can be easier to organise than a workshop, but people can be apathetic about questionnaires which are seen as extra paperwork or a tick-box exercise. Messaging is key here. People need to know and feel that the work is important, and that their contribution will have a direct impact on the school.

The third method I am going to suggest is a smaller version of the workshop outlined above. If you feel that your school is not ready for such a big commitment, or your staff are not ready to have such raw conversations, then selecting a committee can be an effective way to survey a range of voices and opinions. By selecting one or two people from each group (staff, pupils, parents, and governors), you can find out how your school feels and develop a vision statement together. The committee members should be different from the group driving the change in your school, as you need opposing and differing viewpoints to avoid an echo chamber.

Whichever method you choose, not only will you be able to develop a statement that can help to direct your future work, but you will also gather a large amount of information about how your community is feeling about DEIB work. This will help you to foresee both opportunities and barriers and get ahead of them.

Inclusive policies

The bit that I am sure you all love is finally here: policies. (Please do not skip to the next chapter.) Unfortunately, policies get a bad rap. I have seen schools where there are more policies than members of staff, and you know who reads them? No one. What is the point? However, policies are essential to protect pupils, staff, and parents. Written effectively, they help to maintain clarity and transparency, and they are actually one of the best tools we have for tackling misinformation, bullying, and prejudice.

Effective policies are incredibly important for three reasons:

1. They contribute to a common culture of understanding by stating the school's purpose and values.

2. They keep staff and pupils safe by outlining all procedures clearly for all stakeholders.

3. They provide transparency for the school's approach to LGBTQ+ inclusion.

The key policies that I will address in this chapter include equalities, anti-bullying, curriculum, and relationships and sexuality education. These policy areas can become overwhelming beasts, so this might be a good opportunity for you to ascertain whether you can combine certain policies, bin some entirely, or strip them back to their bare essentials. No one needs to be reading *War and Peace* to find out where they should be recording a bullying incident.

I will discuss what these policies should include and why they are important. You might have gathered that I do not like ticking boxes, but this is one area where a list can help because it can be easy to miss things out or put in a lot that is not needed.

This exercise can also help you to triangulate between policies. Although you should not replicate information in different policies, they should be consistent in their use of language and cross-refer to each other. For this reason, I would always advise that these policies are reviewed at the same time.

Equalities policy

An effective equalities policy should specifically address LGBTQ+ inclusion, outlining clear guidelines and support mechanisms for pupils who come out. Schools should establish a safe and confidential process for pupils to disclose their sexual orientation or gender identity. Staff members, especially those in pastoral care roles, must be trained to handle such disclosures with sensitivity and discretion. The policy should make clear that any information shared by pupils is kept confidential unless there is a safeguarding concern.

It can also be helpful to include your position on providing gender-neutral facilities and school uniforms.

Depending on where your school is located, guidance around gender-neutral and same-sex facilities may differ. However, when deciding whether to provide same-sex or unisex facilities, you may want to consider the following questions:

✦ What are the key concerns around safety, accessibility, privacy, and bullying in our current toilets?

✚ How can we ensure that our toilets are inclusive for all learners, including trans, non-binary, and neurodivergent learners?

✚ Would unisex toilets create safeguarding risks, and how could we manage them?

✚ What practical factors (e.g. space, cost, maintenance, privacy) need to be considered?

✚ How does our decision reflect our school's values on inclusivity and equality?

✚ How will we involve learners, staff, and parents in the decision and review its impact?

For most schools that implement unisex toilets, it may also be prudent to keep some same-sex facilities. Not all pupils will be comfortable with unisex toilets, certainly in the short term, and their feelings should also be considered.

School uniform policies impact all pupils, not just those who are gender diverse. They particularly affect girls, pupils from different socio-economic backgrounds, those with sensory sensitivities, and learners from various cultural and religious backgrounds. When reviewing your uniform options to ensure they are inclusive and flexible for everyone, you may want to consider the following questions:

✚ How can you ensure that all learners have the freedom to wear a uniform that aligns with their identity while maintaining a cohesive school appearance?

✚ Are any of your current uniform expectations based on outdated gender norms rather than practical or educational reasons?

✚ How do your uniform policies support the comfort, confidence, and well-being of all learners, including trans, non-binary, and neurodivergent learners, as well as those with sensory needs or religious dress requirements?

✚ What practical factors (e.g. cost, accessibility, weather, cultural considerations) need to be taken into account?

✚ How does your approach to uniform reflect your school's commitment to inclusivity, equality, and learner autonomy?

✛ How will you involve learners, staff, and parents in shaping your uniform policy and ensure that it remains inclusive over time?

By making your stance on these areas clear in your equality policy, you are not only making expectations straightforward for the community to understand, but you are also stating outright that these decisions are rooted in the need for equity and equality.

Your equality policy should:

✛ Name the protected characteristics.

✛ Identify why equalities work is important to your school.

✛ Outline how your processes support the recruitment of a diverse workforce.

✛ Refer to your anti-bullying policy for how to deal with bullying incidents.

✛ Outline what your policy is for when a pupil comes out, particularly around when and how parents will be informed.

✛ State your school's position on when and if a pupil's preferred name and pronouns will be updated on the register.

✛ Outline pupil access to same-sex facilities, such as toilets and changing rooms, if they identify as non-binary or are transgender.

Anti-bullying policy

You already know that LGBTQ+ pupils are at a high risk from bullying. I hate to say it, but too often anti-bullying policies are produced as a paperwork exercise and not as a robust tool for protecting pupils and tackling harassment and discrimination. This policy must clearly define bullying in all its forms, including homophobic, biphobic, and transphobic bullying. It should outline the procedures for reporting and recording incidents, ensuring that all reports are taken seriously and investigated promptly. I visit far too many schools where LGBTQ+ phobic incidents are not given the same prominence as other prejudicial incidents, such as racism, so the policy needs to make clear that prejudice of any kind will be taken as seriously as any other.

In addition to staff recording incidents, it is often useful to implement an anonymous reporting system that allows pupils to report bullying without fear of retaliation. You will need to treat these reports with sensitivity, of course, in case untruthful incidents are logged, but it can help school leaders to gain a true picture of behaviour in the school. After all, you cannot be everywhere at once. How a self-reporting system will be used should be outlined clearly in your policy.

Your anti-bullying policy should:

✚ Give a clear definition of bullying.

✚ Refer to your equalities policy and the importance of supporting minority and under-represented groups.

✚ Ensure that all protected characteristics are given equal weighting, and that one characteristic is not protected more than any other.

✚ Make clear that the use of 'gay' or 'queer' as pejorative terms is a form of bullying, even if not directed at an LGBTQ+ individual.

✚ Supply a flowchart or process for what should happen if a member of staff witnesses an incident of bullying.

✚ Provide a clear process for recording and reporting incidents, including how logged incidents are named and tagged.

✚ Identify how records are transferred between schools.

Curriculum policy

Sometimes produced as a handbook rather than a policy, an inclusive curriculum policy gives all staff a consistent message about how to improve the inclusivity and diversity of the curriculum. This policy should outline expectations for the inclusion of diverse role models, books, and history. It may also address issues related to gender and sexuality in personal, social, health, and economic (PSHE) education, although this may be covered in the relationships and sex education (RSE) policy; if so, it does not need to be repeated.

As well as featuring diverse role models and narratives, an inclusive curriculum should also provide pupils with a broad range of perspectives and experiences. Teaching materials should avoid stereotypes and be inclusive of different family structures and relationships. Schools should also provide opportunities for pupils to engage in discussions about diversity, inclusion, and respect, helping to foster critical thinking and empathy. The curriculum policy is an ideal vehicle for ensuring that diversity and inclusion are embedded in the curriculum rather than a bolt-on.

Your curriculum policy should:

✚ Identify the importance of representing diverse individuals and communities.

✚ Make clear the importance of challenging all stereotypes in society.

✚ Explain your approach to ensuring a representative curriculum.

✚ Outline how you will ensure the age-appropriate introduction of LGBTQ+ terminology and concepts.

Relationships and sexuality education policy

The title of this policy may differ depending on your region, but it should support and hold to account staff and help parents to understand how RSE, RSHE (relationships, sex, and health education), or PSHE are delivered in your school.

This policy should explain how vocabulary will be introduced throughout the school and what the procedures are for parents wanting to request the withdrawal of their child from lessons. The legislation surrounding this varies significantly across the UK, so your policy should reflect the relevant government guidance and statutory requirements.

In secondary schools, there should be references to how you will make sex education inclusive – for example, when introducing contraception and sexually transmitted infection (STIs), and how you will ensure that this is inclusive of LGBTQ+ identities.

Your RSE policy should:

✚ Explain why RSE is important.

✚ Outline how RSE is taught through the school and whether this will be from a specialist teacher, a form tutor, or both.

- Outline where parents can access curriculum plans and resources.
- Make clear your policy for the withdrawal of pupils from lessons.
- Outline how sex education is LGBTQ+ inclusive.

Policies that work *for* you

All too often, we create policies because we have to rather than because they are useful documents that protect, inform, and educate. The key question to ask is: does a particular policy work for you? If it does not actively support pupils and make staff more confident in fostering an inclusive environment, then it needs to change. An effective policy is not just about meeting expectations – it is about making your school a better place for every pupil. Take the time to reflect on the following questions: does your policy truly support all pupils? How do you know it is working? What more could be done? Policies are powerful when they drive real action, and every school should ensure they do just that.

You should also check for duplication; it is far more efficient for policies to reference each other rather than duplicating content. Likewise, you may want to consider how the information can be summarised in documents such as staff handbooks and the school prospectus. This can allow people to get the information they need without reading the entire policy.

Finally, policies should be a living part of school life. To make this a reality, they need to be visible and actionable. Regular reviews with staff, pupils, and families ensure that they remain relevant and effective. Policies should also be embedded in the wider school culture – linked to values, reinforced in everyday decision-making, and supported by clear reporting mechanisms, so learners and staff know how to raise concerns and trust they will be addressed. If they are only referred to once every three years, then they are not making a discernible impact on your school.

Building on strong foundations

It can be tempting to skip this step of creating a vision and reviewing policies. But establishing these foundations ensures that your school has a clear direction moving forward and that both pupils and staff are protected by well-defined guidelines. A strong vision statement helps everyone – staff, pupils, and the wider school community – understand the purpose and goals of your diversity and inclusion work. Clear, up-to-date policies provide a framework that supports decision-making, protects individuals, and fosters a culture of respect and belonging.

Without these foundational elements, diversity initiatives risk being inconsistent, reactive, or lacking long-term impact. By investing time in this stage, schools can create an environment where meaningful change can take place. It also ensures that diversity work is not just a series of one-off activities but part of a strategic and embedded approach. Once these foundations are in place, you can move ahead with confidence, knowing that your efforts are aligned with a shared vision and supported by robust policies that promote inclusion for all.

Chapter 5

Two Peas in a Pod: Pastoral Care and Provision

. . . .

Oh dear, it is time to tell my coming out story. Both morti-fying and hilarious, this shows what can happen when people try to do the right thing but don't understand how important it is to do it in their own time and on their own terms.

Shortly after I had left university and had moved around vari-ous houses, I was invited to have dinner with my parents one evening. My sister and I have talked about this night only recently, and I find it fascinating that we have different recol-lections of what happened – a very common occurrence when people are recalling times of trauma. After finishing dinner, I left the room briefly. When I came back, I was presented with a semicircle of family members. To my horror, my dad had been on a laptop that I'd left at home and had seen the web-sites and chatrooms I'd visited; yes, it is exactly what you're thinking. And then he asked me if I was gay. There was no warning, and it certainly wasn't the end of the evening that I had been expecting.

Confronted in this way, I immediately said no, which damaged our relationship for several months. This is because I was embarrassed and wasn't ready to say anything yet. Unless there is a clear safeguarding risk, no one should be forced to come out. It should be their choice and their journey.

Afterwards, I remember being in my sister's car as she drove me to a local shop and her saying that I should talk when I was ready. This kindness made it so much easier, and it wasn't long after that I began to come out to other people. It happened gradually by speaking to various groups of friends at different times and garnering reactions ranging from shock to messages of 'Yeah, we knew all along.'

Finally, being able to be honest about my feelings and myself was certainly a step in the right direction. While my journey was far from over, I can honestly say that a weight was lifted from my shoulders, which allowed me to explore who the real Ian was – because, until that time, I had no idea.

. . . .

Consistency is the cornerstone of an inclusive school. Without it, the messages your pupils receive about their value and safety can become fragmented and unclear, leading to confusion and alienation. When your staff share a unified approach to inclusion, this will build trust and ensure that every pupil experiences the same support, no matter who they interact with. This is why inspectors ask the same safeguarding questions to multiple staff members. They are looking for a culture where everyone understands their role in protecting and supporting pupils. The same principle applies to LGBTQ+ inclusion: consistency reassures pupils that their identities and experiences are respected across every aspect of school life.

At the heart of consistency lies a set of shared principles. Whether we are talking about pastoral care or the curriculum, common principles should guide every action, decision, and interaction within the school. They provide the foundation for addressing biases, promoting diversity, and ensuring that no child feels excluded or unseen. Without clear principles, well-meaning actions can become superficial or even counterproductive. The vision statement you created in the previous chapter will support this and guide the work you do.

Pastoral care plays a crucial role in creating an inclusive environment. It often serves as the first point of contact for pupils seeking help, offering a vital safety net for those navigating challenges related to identity, relationships, or discrimination. While specific pastoral teams might take the lead, effective pastoral care requires every member of staff to take ownership of the well-being and inclusion of pupils. Teachers, teaching assistants, office staff, and school leaders all have a role to play in fostering a school culture where every child feels safe, valued, and supported. This shared responsibility ensures that inclusion is not confined to one team or area but is felt consistently throughout the school. Pupils should know that no matter who they approach, they will find understanding, empathy, and actionable support.

This is also true of the curriculum. Staff should understand that true inclusion does not just lie with the PSHE team or diversity leads but with all staff. A truly inclusive curriculum is developed through everyone knowing how they can contribute to the whole.

In this chapter, we will explore how schools can integrate LGBTQ+ inclusion into the curriculum in an age-appropriate way, while also challenging stereotypes, and how pastoral care and curriculum design can work together to create a cohesive and supportive environment. We will also examine how to build a culture of consistency through shared understanding, clear policies, and effective training, ensuring that inclusion is deeply embedded in every part of school life.

Bullying is so gay

'What did you think of that film last night? Wasn't it so straight?'

Would anyone ever say this? Nope, it does not even really make sense. But take a moment to reflect on why not. The answer is simple: society does not see being straight in a negative way. I am now going to change it:

'What did you think of that film last night? Wasn't it so gay?'

Now, all of a sudden, although it is not nice to read, you understand what it means. Our society understands the word 'gay' as a negative term, which results in making it more challenging for gay young people to be themselves because their very identity is labelled as a deficiency.

I am sure everyone reading this would agree that we should take a zero-tolerance approach to all bullying in schools. But the reality is that we still see a large amount of LGBTQ+ phobic bullying in schools, with up to 87% of LGBT+ pupils being bullied in schools across the world.[1] In the previous chapter, I took you through how to ensure that your policies are clear about the definition of bullying and the process of challenging it. But this process will falter if some staff are not clear on whether certain actions or words are homophobic in nature.

In primary schools, rather than overt homophobia, there is a prevalence of the use of the word 'gay' as a derogatory term – for example, 'That is so gay.' As all too often this is not tackled quickly enough, this then evolves in secondary schools into more direct homophobic comments. But why is homophobia still so common, and why have we not eradicated the use of the word 'gay' as a term of abuse?

When I go into schools, I always ask the following three questions – in this order:

1. What can you tell me about racism in this school?

2. What can you tell me about homophobia in this school?

3. What can you tell me about the use of the word 'gay' as an insult in this school?

The responses are fascinating. I would urge you to do the same if you really want to find out why gay is being used as a derogatory term. In almost every single school I have visited, there is a common pattern that explains why gay as a negative term has not gone away.

In response to my first question, every school always make clear how seriously they are tackling racism, and that although racist language occurs, there are clear procedures and consequences. To the second, most will deny that there is any homophobia or that it is rare. When I ask my final question, the mood usually shifts. I often get comments such as, 'Well, they aren't aiming it at anyone,' 'They don't mean it,' or 'They don't know what it means.' But my biggest concern is about how the use of the word is addressed. Ask yourself, are you treating this with the same seriousness as directed homophobia or racist language? If not, why not?

---

1   N. Moyano and M. d. M. Sánchez-Fuentes, Homophobic Bullying at Schools: A Systematic Review of Research, Prevalence, School-Related Predictors and Consequences, *Aggression and Violent Behavior*, 53 (2020): 101441. https://doi.org/10.1016/j.avb.2020.101441.

Let us consider why the use of gay is so bad if it is not used to directly abuse a gay person. Think about if you were a teenage boy worried about coming out and struggling to come to terms with your identity. If the people around you (and maybe even you) are using gay in this way, it gives the message that being gay is wrong or bad. That is only going to add to your anxiety about who you are and discourage you from coming out. It also gives other people permission to talk about being gay and other LGBTQ+ identities in a negative way.

The only way to tackle the harmful use of this word is through a whole-school approach where the reasons for not using it in this way are made very clear to pupils. It is equally important that every member of staff enforces this approach, so the pupils understand that this is the view of the school and not just individual teachers.

A two-pronged approach is required: education and consequence. Too often, schools pursue one and not the other. After an incident, if a pupil is educated on why it is wrong but does not receive a consequence, they are given the message that it is wrong, but that you will tolerate it in your school. If they receive a consequence but no education, they may not understand why it is wrong and there will be no long-term change.

When an incident occurs, it is essential that all staff are empowered to act immediately. The pupil using the word must be told straight away that it is unacceptable. They must then face a consequence and be educated on the meaning of the word and the impact that using it in a negative way can have. This should then be recorded as a homophobic incident. I hate to be blunt here, but if your school is not recording this as homophobia, then you are giving a pass to people to say that it is acceptable.

You might notice that this is the same process as tackling bullying. And it should be. All staff need to understand that using the word 'gay' negatively is prejudice, and until this is viewed with the seriousness it should be, its use as a pejorative term will not stop.

But I did not mean it?

I am going to play devil's advocate here and suggest that the first time a pupil uses a word in a pejorative way, it may be out of genuine ignorance of what the word means. So, on this occasion, for whatever type of discrimination, the most important point is to educate them on why it is wrong to use the word in that way. After this, it can no longer be an excuse. If we continually allow pupils to feign ignorance, then we are giving them a way out of a consequence.

If you have a widespread issue with particular words, the most effective way to deal with it is a whole-school approach. Providing staff training (to all staff) and pupil workshops/assemblies making it clear that this behaviour must stop is the best way to avoid any wiggle room. The most commonly forgotten group here is lunch-time and break-time supervisors. Most schools report that most of these issues occur outside of lessons, so if our break-time supervisors are not receiving the same training or delivering the same expectations, it cannot be any surprise that this behaviour is prevalent then.

Out of the closet

It can be easy to overlook the reasons why people come out. If you are straight or cisgender, you do not need to come out, as your sexual or gender identity is the same as more than 90% of the population. To come out as straight, for example, would be odd as it is what people would expect. But when you are in a minority, especially if it is not visible, you will want to come out so that you do not feel that you have to hide who you are. Now, I long for the days when coming out is no longer a thing, and everyone just accepts that people are who they are, but we do not live in that world.

Coming out is not something that most people decide to do on a whim. It is the culmination of a long period of self-reflection, self-acceptance, and, in many cases, a big dollop of bravery. Many people worry that they will be viewed differently, treated badly, or even rejected. It can take a lot of courage, so to be pressured into that situation can be very traumatic.

Pupils do not tend to come out in school first, with only around one in four coming out to a teacher.[2] It is more than likely that most people around a child or young person already know. Sorry teachers – we are far down the priority list after friends and family! Occasionally, school staff will be among the first to know, so it is essential that your staff are trained on what to do. The biggest concern that staff have when I train them is knowing what to say and who you are allowed to tell. There are three things I would like you to remember if a young person comes out to you:

1. It is a privilege that they have trusted you enough to come out.

2. They are telling you for a reason.

3. Being LGBTQ+ is not a safeguarding issue.

First, it is vital that we thank the young person for telling us. It has taken a lot for them to be honest, so as long as you are not being patronising, thanking them makes it clear that you appreciate it.

Next, listen to what they are saying. Think about why they are telling you. It could be because they just want you to know, or it might be because they need to get something across. Perhaps they need help in accepting their identity, or they are nervous about telling people, or they are experiencing bullying. Try not to pressure them. Ask open questions and tread the line between being interested but not making them feel interrogated. This is not a cross-examination. Following on from this, you might need to take some action, but in most cases knowing is enough.

Finally, ask who knows and who they want to know. This is not your piece of information to share, so the young person should have control over who knows and when they find out. The chances are, the answer will be 'everyone', but in the rare instance when they are not ready to tell everyone yet, careful thought should go into how we protect their confidentiality, while also safeguarding them.

2   Just Like Us, *Positive Futures: How Supporting LGBT+ Young People Enables Them to Thrive in Adulthood* (2023), p. 16. Available at: https://www.justlikeus.org/wp-content/uploads/2023/05/Positive-Futures-report-by-Just-Like-Us-compressed-for-mobile.pdf.

Once they have come out, usually there is nothing more to do but crack on with life. You might want to check in on them every now and again to see how they are. But for most young people, once they have come out, they just want to get on with their life.

However, there are certain circumstances when you will need to take additional action. I do not want to scare you, especially as these have all happened in schools I have worked with, but it is better to be prepared for the worst and it never happens than to be unprepared.

The first rule when thinking about this issue is that safeguarding must come first. Although we should respect the confidentiality of young people and let them come out in their own time, this cannot come at the expense of their safety. Here are some examples where safeguarding should override confidentiality:

+ They are being bullied.

+ They are at risk of self-harming.

+ Their mental health is declining.

+ They are on adult dating apps.

+ They are having a relationship with an adult.

In all these instances, you should follow your school's safeguarding procedures. Generally, this would mean explaining to the young person that you need to support them and that this will involve talking to their parents.

When deciding what to do, ask yourself these questions:

+ Why do they not want some people to know?

+ Are they at risk?

+ What support do they need to come out publicly?

It can be helpful to discuss the scenarios below during staff train-ing, so that everyone has a clear understanding of what to do. These situations are all based on actual events in schools, and although they are rare, it can be useful to check that everyone understands what policies and procedures are in place.

A pupil comes out to you, but they do not want their parents to know because they are not ready. They ask you to keep it to yourself.

The first thing we need to find out is why they do not want their parents to know. In the vast majority of circumstances, it is probably that they are not ready to tell them yet, and that is fine. People need time to accept their identity and should be given the space they need to share this information.

However, if there is any concern about their well-being, your safeguarding procedures should take precedence. For example, if the pupil said they were afraid that they were going to be hurt by a family member, that they were self-harming, or that they were going to be kicked out of their home, then this is a safeguarding concern, and you would follow the necessary procedures. At every point, you would be keeping the young person informed and ensuring that they understood that you need to disclose their identity for their own safety.

A member of staff comes into the staffroom and starts to talk about a supply teacher who has told them in confidence that they are transgender. They say that they have never met someone like that before.

Although this member of staff may not deliberately mean to cause harm, they have reduced an individual's life to gossip and shared information that may not be public. Although someone's identity is not something to be ashamed of, it is also not our business to share information that is not ours to dispense. This member of staff needs to be reminded that they should respect others' confidentiality and that other people's identities should not be a source of gossip.

An autistic pupil has come into school and told everyone they have transitioned. They have asked other pupils to use their new names and pronouns, but not everyone is using them. Some pupils have begun to target them with upsetting comments, and they are becoming increasingly distraught.

Their parents do not know about the transition and the pupil does not want them to know.

This is quite a complex issue, but it comes down to one question: is the pupil at risk? When we look at the fact that they are potentially being bullied and that their mental health is possibly being damaged by the reactions of others, then the answer is yes. In this case, safeguarding would override their wish for confidentiality and the parents would need to be informed. I would always recommend that the pupil is kept informed, but our foremost responsibility is for their well-being. The pupil has not understood what a complicated journey transitioning is, so we need to give them the help and support they require to explore their identity without putting themselves at risk. There is also a need to educate the rest of the school because, regardless of how poorly the transition was executed, there is never any excuse for bullying or name-calling.

Coming out is a tremendously personal experience, and if pupils are comfortable coming out in your school then you should be proud that you have created an environment that is supportive and safe. Even though we have covered a lot of worst-case scenarios here, I want to end on a positive note: most people who come out just want to live their lives. They do not want drama, and they do not want to be treated differently; they just want to live as themselves and be happy.

Pastoral care

The reality of coming out and coming to terms with being LGBTQ+ is that some young people will struggle with their identity more than others. Even if you have the most inclusive school environment, the most accepting staff, and the most diverse curriculum, LGBTQ+ people are still a minority group and so going on the journey to true acceptance will be challenging for some.

While there are some who will come out and not need any additional support, others will find it difficult in different ways. Some will not come out in public as they are afraid of the reaction (and maybe have not yet accepted it themselves). Some people's identity may conflict with their religious beliefs and/or cultural traditions, and this can lead to them hiding their identity or risking exclusion from their community. The complexities surrounding coming out are very intricate, so you will often need to assess individuals on a case-by-case basis to ascertain what support they need, if anything.

There have been many times when I have walked into a secondary school and been shown the most beautiful display of LGBTQ+ posters and leaflets, where I am told that pupils are directed to the nurse's office who offers guidance to LGBTQ+ pupils, and where I have been assured that the school has done a great deal of inclusivity work with their community. And then I speak to the pupils ... who tell me they have no idea that any of this exists.

When we are thinking about pastoral care, it is not only about *what* we offer but *how* we communicate the services and provision. You should identify whether these resources are well-publicised, accessible, and staffed by individuals trained in LGBTQ+ support. It is vital to speak to your pupils about their views on what is available, as our well-intentioned initiatives can sometimes be missed by the pupils who need them the most.

In primary schools, it is unlikely that these services will be visible to pupils, but they should still be there in policies and handbooks.

Consider creating a pathway, as you would for children with additional learning needs, setting out where pupils can go for support in your school and where they can access support locally. There are amazing LGBTQ+ organisations in most areas that will be able to provide advice or support, but you might not know they exist until you look.

What to teach and when

When schools are thinking about the principles of an inclusive curriculum, one of the concerns that many people have is when exactly do you begin to talk about LGBTQ+ concepts, and how do you ensure that the work is age-appropriate.

If I asked to you break down how to teach addition or when to teach different parts of grammar into year groups for the average pupil, I bet you would be pretty confident. There are several reasons for this: you can fall back on your own memories of school, it was probably covered in your teacher training, and there are a lot of resources out there mapping these subjects. But come to inclusion and diversity and suddenly you might be feeling nervous about what to teach and when. When do we start using LGBTQ+ vocabulary? When is it okay to teach about same-sex relationships? What exactly does that look like in different year groups in the school? Some of the anxiety in this area stems from the fact that most of us never had this type of education in school, and there is also a lot of misinformation and scaremongering on social media.

In the rest of this chapter, I am going to break down exactly what I think should be taught and when. However, this is not a definitive scheme of work, and you should feel empowered to make changes based on your own setting and community.

The introduction of LGBTQ+ vocabulary

Some people suggest that the earlier you introduce new vocabulary, the better as it can prevent stigma. Although this is true, it ignores language development and the potential for misconceptions to creep in. We also need to consider why it might be beneficial to bring in words at different stages.

Take the example of my son. He was 8 when he learned the word 'gay', for the simple reason that he did not need to use it beforehand. It was only when he overheard it in a conversation that I explained what it meant. It is not about being afraid of certain words but considering whether we are introducing them for the right reasons.

If we introduce language too early, there is a risk of misunderstanding. Take the label 'asexual'. I have seen primary resources that define this as someone who does not want a romantic relationship. This is incorrect: by simplifying the definition down to age-appropriate terms, it has lost its meaning. To explain what being asexual is, you would need to talk about sexual attraction and sexual intercourse outside of conception, both of which would be inappropriate in primary school. Withholding certain language until a later date does not make it taboo but instead ensures that it is introduced at a suitable stage.

The same issue applies to language around transgender and non-binary identities. Although children gain a strong sense of gender at around the age of 3,[3] this does not necessarily mean they can articulate this through language or that they understand the concepts outside of their own sphere of comprehension. Just because children know what boys and girls are does not mean that they understand the difference between sex and gender. Without this understanding, discussing transgender identities often becomes about the way people look or male and female stereo- types. This could easily result in those stereotypes being reinforced, or even new ones being created, which could not only confuse children but also diminish what it means to be transgender or non-binary.

While words such as gay or lesbian should not be prohibited, if there is no clear reason to talk about them before pupils can under- stand the concepts, then we need to consider the rationale for introducing them. Labels can be useful, but they can also be a hin- drance. Especially in the earlier years of school, our focus should be on tackling stereotypes and helping children to accept each other for who they are rather than who they are 'meant' to be.

The following guide outlines when you might consider introducing vocabulary for each age group, but you must always do what is right for your children and your community.

Age 0–3

In the early years, you may feel that LGBTQ+ language is unneces- sary and that pupils' understanding of LGBTQ+ communities can be limited to recognising that some children have two mums or two dads. However, you may feel that you would like to introduce the words 'gay' and 'lesbian' to avoid stigma later on. Even if you decide to postpone formally introducing LGBTQ+ vocabulary, your

---

3   C. L. Martin and D. N. Ruble, Patterns of Gender Development, *Annual Review of Psychology*, 61 (2010): 353–381. https://doi.org/10.1146/annurev.psych.093008.100511.

staff should not be afraid of using the words in conversation or shutting children down if they use them. These words should never be taboo.

Age 3–7

As with the early years, you may feel that the most important issue here is representation rather than the express teaching of language. Pupils at this age learn through hearing and seeing words repeatedly and in different contexts. Simply dropping in lesbian and gay when talking about same-sex families can help to reduce stigma and introduce the words in a very natural way.

Age 8–11

This is when most schools will formally introduce LGB vocabulary, generally through talking about role models. For example, when describing role models in sport, you can mention in passing that a particular athlete is gay. There is no need to do an entire lesson about LGBTQ+ role models. This can create an 'us and them' view, whereas what we want to do is show representation as part of the fabric of our society. This is generally the age when gay will start to be used as a pejorative term, so you may need specific anti-bullying lessons on this and similar words.

Age 11–16

When you introduce terminology around transgender and non-binary identities will depend on your pupils and what you feel is best for your school, but there is a general consensus that age 11 or 12 is when many pupils begin to become more aware of their identity. At this stage, we can also bring in language around asexuality, which is particularly important when talking about consent and appropriate relationships. For asexual teenagers, talking about asexuality can help to alleviate the pressure they may feel to have sex and inform others about the importance of respecting consent.

You may feel that in your school you want to introduce language around intersex or differences in sex development. This could potentially take place during lessons around sexual development, but it should always be taught sensitively, so if there are intersex pupils in the room or people with relatives who are intersex, they are not made to feel that it is something to be ashamed of.

The most important factor when deciding when to introduce LGBTQ+ vocabulary is to be aware of why you are introducing the words at a particular stage. We live in a world where schools are sometimes challenged on these topics, so you must be able to explain your rationale. You also need to be flexible so that people are not afraid to use certain words, and if the need arises, you can change your plans for an individual cohort.

The 'gay lesson'

I am going to make a big plea here. Please do not do what I often refer to as the 'gay lesson', which is all about vocabulary and the children writing down meanings for words such as lesbian, gay, bisexual, and so on. Not only is this a really dull lesson and goes against the research on the effective teaching of vocabulary, but it also creates the idea that these people are somehow different.

Good morning class. Look at this picture – this is a gay. Look at what they are wearing, look at their hair, look at the jobs they are doing. But I assure you, they are normal. I might be doing a one-off lesson talking about the gays, but they are definitely part of our society just like everyone else. Now, let's write out a list of LGBTQ+ vocabulary and what the words mean because that is the best way to learn new words.

Okay, I might be exaggerating a tiny bit, but there are some grains of truth here in how LGBTQ+ role models and diversity are often represented in the curriculum. By pointing out that some people are different, we immediately create the idea that they are some-how not normal. At this point, I would like to thank Sue Sanders (co-founder of LGBT+ History Month) for teaching me the word 'usualise'. If we use the word 'normal' to describe any minority or under-represented group, we are suggesting that the alternative is abnormal, which very much feeds into prejudiced views. Instead, by taking about usualising, we are saying that these identities are unusual in our communities, which they often are. I also like using the words 'common' and 'uncommon'. Whatever word you choose to use, please avoid normal. And if you have a worksheet for the children to write in definitions for LGBTQ+ words, I implore you to bin it and never speak of it again!

It is far more effective to introduce this language naturally when it comes up in a relevant context. For example, if you are looking at sports role models, you can casually mention that one of them is a lesbian and, if necessary, explain what that means. The lesson is not about lesbians, it is about sports, which is as it should be. If we want to usualise LGBTQ+ identities, then we must show that LGBTQ+ people are part of the fabric of society and not a separate category.

Exploring the history of LGBTQ+ rights can be incredibly interesting and important in understanding modern contexts for equality. You may want to do a project on the Stonewall riots, for example. However, all too often I see this taught as a one-off lesson. For young people to really understand this subject, they need to learn about the gay and lesbian rights movement in the context of the United States in the 1960s and 1970s. Do they understand the politics and cultural context of the time? Do they know what led up to the Stonewall riots? Do they know what other major events were going on in the United States at the time? If we want to get the most out of these topics, teaching them as standalone lessons not only risks them becoming a tick-box exercise, but also the pupils do not get as much out of it as they potentially could.

'Queering' the subjects

Embedding the teaching of LGBTQ+ identities and communities in subjects should not be about forcing them in but about recognising the actual world we live in. I was working in a school recently where a class was learning about Frida Kahlo. They did an amazing in-depth project into much of her history, life, and activism, but there was one thing missing: there was not one mention of her being bisexual or how she challenged gender norms. Initially, you might wonder why this matters, but Kahlo's art, life, and activism were significantly shaped by her love life. Her art pushed the boundaries of gender norms, and for her to live as openly as she did was remarkable for the time.

The problem with excluding these parts of Kahlo's life is that we are not actually telling her true story. Of course, we have to ensure that we are being age-appropriate – I am not suggesting we would talk about her infidelity in primary school – but discussing her bisexuality from Year 6 onwards should not cause any issues. The following suggestions for LGBTQ+ inclusion in different subjects are not about jamming inclusion into the curriculum but representing the real world in an age-appropriate and accessible way.

English

Looking at the books we use is a natural place to identify how inclusive a school is. In Chapter 6, we will examine representation, and English is arguably the most important subject for this. Through books, we can make sure that every pupil sees a version of themselves, but that they also encounter and learn about people who are different from them.

History

History lends itself perfectly to LGBTQ+ inclusion in some ways, but it can also be very challenging to get it right. There are some obvious areas to include in the curriculum. The Stonewall riots, Section 28, and the introduction of same-sex rights are key points in LGBTQ+ history and should appear in all secondary history curricula as they have directly or indirectly affected all our lives. There can also be some fascinating investigations into characters in history with an LGBTQ+ lens, such as Virginia Woolf or Edward II. However, these should only be explored at an age-appropriate time for the pupils and by a confident practitioner who is prepared for the open-ended discussions and range of opinions and questions that may emerge.

Mathematics

Maths teachers often worry about how to be LGBTQ+ inclusive because, let us face it, 1 + 1 = 2 no matter if you are gay or straight. One option would be to make word problems as diverse as possible by talking about same-sex couples, using inclusive names, and try-ing not to reinforce stereotypes, but, in reality, that is not going to make an enormous amount of difference. Where mathematics can support LGBTQ+ inclusion is, where relevant, by learning about LGBTQ+ mathematicians who challenged boundaries. This does not need to be a big project, or even an entire lesson, but if teachers have this knowledge then these diverse role models can be intro-duced organically through classroom discussions.

Politics

Politics has had a profound impact on LGBTQ+ rights. It can be an influential definer in many premierships. When looking at the Margaret Thatcher years, it would be exclusionary not to discuss Section 28 as it impacted on every single pupil between 1988 and 2003 in different ways. It is also important to recognise the com-plexity of these years and not to suggest a right or wrong view. The decisions politicians make to change equal rights legislation are shaped by the views and culture of the time, so it is essential that any work reflects this.

Science

Like mathematics, there is an opportunity to learn about diverse scientists, particularly those who challenged gender norms. There are many theories about Leonardo da Vinci being gay, for example, but we have to be careful that we are not suggesting that he was definitely gay; only he would know and we can only speculate. Learning about reproduction can also be an opportunity to explain how heterosexual and homosexual couples may have children through IVF or surrogacy.

Inclusive sex education

Over the years, I have had numerous conversations with many of my gay friends about the inadequate sex education we received in school. While the girls had sessions about menstruation, the boys were given an extra hour of break time (we did not complain at the time). What transpired during that session remained a mystery to us boys, and fanciful theories circulated among us. That was pretty much it. Apart from a very brief mention of conception in science, we were left to fend for ourselves. The issue with a lack of sex education is that young people often look for it from unreliable sources, such as peers, the internet, or pornography.

Today's secondary school sex education is much more comprehensive, covering a wide range of topics essential for sexual health. However, traditional programmes often focus on conception and heterosexual relationships, leaving out LGBTQ+ experiences. This oversight can be risky for LGBTQ+ individuals as they miss out on crucial information, leading to higher chances of discrimination, mental health issues, and risky behaviours.

From my own experience, I can attest to the dangers of this gap in education. Without proper guidance, I had to navigate my sexual health through trial and error. The lack of education left me vulnerable to misinformation and potential harm – a situation that many in the LGBTQ+ community unfortunately share.

In the UK, although most young people get their information about sexual health from school, many LGBTQ+ pupils learn about it from the internet and social media.[4] Because of the prevalence of poor information online, there are huge risks associated with this, including an increased risk of contracting STIs, physical injury, and being subjected to controlling or coercive behaviour. For example, many schools will teach pupils about the use of contraception, but this will be focused on heterosexual couples. When your pupils receive education on using condoms, for example, are they also taught how to use lubricants if they are going to be having anal sex as part of a male-to-male physical relationship? We need to

---

4 Sex Education Forum, *Young People's RSE Poll 2024* (11 April 2024). Available at: https://www.sexeducationforum.org.uk/sites/default/files/field/attachment/Young%20Peoples%20RSE%20Poll%202024%20-%20Report.pdf.

usualise conversations about safe sex to include same-sex couples, so that all young people have the information they need to keep safe.

This can be another area where there is a knowledge gap. As many teachers will not have received inclusive sex education themselves when in school and will not have lived experience of all areas of inclusive intercourse, training and professional development is vital.

It is essential to recognise the unique needs of the LGBTQ+ community within sex education to ensure that everyone gets the support and knowledge they need. While sex education alone cannot wave a magic wand and eliminate all the risks associated with sexual behaviour, there is growing evidence that high-quality, inclusive education goes a long way in protecting young people.

Chapter 6

Representation and Role Models

· ·

The next few years were a road to recovery for me. My parents knew that I wasn't right and that I was depressed, but they had no idea about the events that took place before I left university. They paid for therapy for me and, slowly but surely, I started the long process of dealing with all the memories and emotions that had directed my life for so long.

This was the time when I began to accept myself for who I was and unlearn all the negative messages about being gay that had been drilled into me in school. I have always battled with a sense of internalised homophobia; for example, I'm not comfortable seeing two men hold hands on the street. It is not something that is talked about enough, and there is a shame in much of the LGBTQ+ community about feeling this way. But if you have been told for all your formative years that being LGBTQ+ is wrong, or even if people just don't talk about it, it is bound to have an impact on the way you feel.

In 2004, after being made redundant from the joyous world of call centres, I needed another job. In an off-chance conversation in a pub where I was doing some part-time work, a head teacher asked if I would volunteer to do some reading with the children. I'd never had any experience with children, and I couldn't imagine anything worse than spending time with a load of snotty kids, but I reluctantly agreed (I had nothing better to do). Within 10 minutes of working in a primary school, I knew that was where I was meant to be. Before I knew it, I was a qualified teacher and working in an amazing primary school in Bargoed, South Wales.

Over the next 17 years, I had a job I loved. But it was also a time of ignorant bliss. For 15 years, I didn't experience any homophobia. As far as I was concerned, gay people were accepted and the days of bullying were long gone. I didn't know that it was still out there. Perhaps part of this was that I surrounded myself with positive people and the schools I worked in were very inclusive places, but perhaps it was also that the world was changing – and not for the better.

· ·

Okay, quick-fire quiz time! Can you give me an example of one of these people who comes from your town, city, or local area: an equal rights activist, an out sports person, a male dancer, and a female football player.

How did you do? I am betting not very well. (If you did, I applaud you and your education). If I asked you to tell me each of these from a national or international stage, I imagine you would find it far easier.

I recently had a conversation with someone about Martin Luther King Jr. In most Western countries, he is a staple in education about equal rights and the civil rights movement. He is an incredible figure but far from the only person who has made a real difference. The issue is not that we learn about King but that we do not learn about other activists and role models. If we live outside of Georgia in the United States and still know about Martin Luther King Jr, why can most of us not name many activists from our own area?

The same applies to LGBTQ+ history. Most pupils learning about the gay and lesbian rights movement of the 1960s and 1970s will hear about the events that took place at the Stonewall Inn in Greenwich Village, New York City. While I am not disputing its importance, why are schools not teaching about the gay and lesbian rights actions in their own country or area?

Part of the reason for this discrepancy is the knowledge gap that I outlined in the Introduction. As a pupil, you were likely taught a limited amount or even no knowledge of diverse history. When you did learn about role models or major events in inclusion, they were likely to be few and far between and nowhere near where your school is located. Therefore, we have a situation where teachers do not have the information they need to teach these topics. This can lead to stereotypical views of history and role models, which do not reflect the complexity of the real situation.

In this chapter, we will find out how to ensure that our representation and role models give a more realistic view of the world, and that the role models we teach about mean something to our children and young people. Although this book focuses mainly on LGBTQ+ inclusion, I am going to discuss wider diversity too, as this is a good opportunity to look at all characteristics and how we can make our environment and the curriculum inclusive for all.

Where do you belong?

It's hard to be what you can't see.

Marian Wright Edelman

We know that one of the most important things for young people's sense of belonging is that they see role models and representations of themselves in school.[1] We are not just considering sexuality here; the same is also true for race, disability, and all other aspects of diversity. Every child deserves to see their family and themselves in the curriculum. When we look at pictures in textbooks, we should see a variety of people who reflect the diversity of our world. Whether that is same-sex parents, single parents, people with hearing aids, people from different religions, and so on, we need to help our children and young people see the world as it is, not a whitewashed, heteronormative, or ableist view of it. Now, we need to be sensible here. If we try to get every single form of disability into every single topic, our planning is quickly going to become untenable and will turn into a tick-box exercise where teachers may actually begin to resent DEIB, and the inclusion will become meaningless. But, where relevant, aim to include this diversity and assess the curriculum on a regular basis to see what has been included. Sometimes, we need to take a step back and look at a few term's work, or even a whole year's work, to see where opportunities were missed and try to include them in the future.

---

1 Just Like Us, *Growing Up LGBT+: The Impact of School, Home and Coronavirus on LGBT+ Young People* (2021). Available at: https://www.justlikeus.org/wp-content/uploads/2021/11/Just-Like-Us-2021-report-Growing-Up-LGBT.pdf.

This type of exercise can give a very quick insight into how representative the curriculum is in your school. However, we must also remember that it will only provide a partial window into how LGBTQ+ issues are being addressed, represented, and integrated within the educational framework.

Visuals around the school

Take a walk around your school and look at the imagery on display. Most likely, you will see imagery of the pupils, the community, and role models. What do the photos of the pupils tell you about your school population? Ensuring a diverse range of imagery of young people is important for two reasons. First, it helps minority or under-represented groups to feel represented in the school and part of the community. Second, it educates majority groups that there are people in your school, and in the wider world, who look different to them. This might appear to be virtue signalling, and it is true that without deeper commitments to diversity this would have little impact, but changing your imagery to be more representative is an easy step to affirming your commitment to diversity.

You will no doubt also have displays and, increasingly, specific displays to demonstrate diversity in your school. While these can be important, it is also imperative that diversity is not boxed into specific tasks, displays, and months.

A story for every pupil

I do not know if it is a teacher thing, or the fact that as a child I so often hid away in books, or that I rediscovered my love for reading during the pandemic, but I love books. I really do. One of my favourite parts of teaching was reading to the children at the end of the day or really getting stuck into a novel to inspire my class's topic work. Books have a magical way of opening doors to worlds we could not imagine before, helping us to see something from someone else's perspective or to realise that we are not alone in the way we look, feel, or are.

Imagine sitting in a classroom, a book open before you, its pages filled with characters embarking on grand adventures, facing challenges, and finding their place in the world. Now, imagine that none of those characters look like you, love like you, or experience the world in the ways that you do. Instead, they all belong to a reality that feels far removed from your own. How does that make you feel? Do you feel seen, valued, and included? Or do you feel invisible, as though your story is not worth telling?

Representation in the books you read is not just about seeing yourself; it is about understanding others. I love the idea of books being windows, mirrors, and doors. They allow us to see ourselves, so we know that we are not alone in this world. They allow us to see into other people's worlds, to empathise with them, and to understand their point of view. They allow us to step outside of our world into someone else's, whether that is to escape our own or to walk a mile in their metaphorical shoes.

The books we use in school say a lot about how we view the world. Historically, books in British schools have not represented the diversity of our world and often present a very White, Christian, ableist, straight view. This narrow lens is a far cry from the multicultural world we live in and misses the opportunity to connect pupils with the richness of different lives and perspectives.

For those of you who have ever felt unseen, finding representation in a book can be life-changing. Imagine being a young person who has just realised that you are different in a way that feels isolating. You might be the only individual in your school who feels this way, or so it seems. Then, one day, you read a story about someone just like you. They navigate similar fears, face similar challenges, and yet they thrive. That story might be the lifeline that reminds you that you are not alone, that you belong, that there is hope.

For others, reading about lives and experiences vastly different from their own can shatter prejudices. It can turn assumptions into understanding. When you read about someone who has faced discrimination, endured hardships, or lived a reality unlike your own, you gain an insight into their humanity. You begin to see the world through their eyes and, in doing so, your heart grows a little bigger. This is the power of representation – it connects us across divides.

In schools, the stories you share carry immense weight. If the books you choose only reflect one kind of story or one kind of person, you unintentionally send a message about whose stories matter and whose do not. You risk teaching young pupils that there is a 'normal' and that everything else is 'other'. But when you include stories from diverse voices, you say: all stories matter, all people matter.

It can feel daunting to begin this process. You may wonder where to start or worry about making mistakes, but the effort is worth it. Ensuring representation in the books you choose means creating a world where every child feels valued. The following pages will equip you with the tools and techniques to help you take these vital steps. Together, we can ensure that every pupil has the opportunity to see themselves and others in the stories they read.

The story comes first

Before you begin to buy boxes of diverse books, consider the quality of the books available. Just because they include inclusive characters or are written by an author from a minority or underrepresented background, does not mean that they are good or that they are right for your school. You need to be selective with the books you choose and be able to justify why you chose them.

When I started teaching, there was little diversity in the books we used. When I did find diversity, it was often stereotypical or focused on teaching about diversity rather than stories that included diverse characters. Things have definitely improved in the last 10 years, with more books about characters from different races and faiths, and the beginnings of seeing families who do not look like the typical 2.4 child family.

The first book I ever bought for my school that featured two dads was written specifically to explain to children that some families have two dads.[2] In 2014, books like this were paving the way for a far more inclusive future, and I am not disparaging the author or publisher at all. To write and publish it was an incredibly brave move in a world that was still reeling from Section 28. But, on reflection, the book was more of a narrative textbook designed to

---

2 C. Robertson, *Two Dads: A Book About Adoption* (N.p.: Sparklypoo Publications, 2014).

teach about the diversity of families than a creative story with positive representation.

While this may have appeared to be a good thing, it now makes me slightly uneasy. My family should not be a subject that needs to be taught. If we talk about same-sex families in this way, what does it say about my son's family, for example? It suggests that we are not (and here is that word again) normal. If we are to truly present diversity in a way such that all families and people have an equal place in society, then representation needs to be more (or, in a way, less) than teaching.

When I look at your school's books, I want to see that diverse characters are just part of the story. They exist in the world. They have flaws. They do not need to be taught about. This applies to all aspects of diversity. We should not just have books that explain why some people are in wheelchairs. We should have books in which a character has an adventure and just happens to be in a wheelchair. Black characters should not always experience racism or be linked to slavery. We should have books where a character has an amazing story and just happens to be Black. Only when we move to this type of representation will our curriculum give the message that our world is diverse, and that is just the way it is.

The other issue with some of these books is that the story comes second to the diversity and representation. This can often manifest in books where the story is not that great. When you open up a book that includes diversity, forget for a moment that there are diverse characters in it. Judge the story and the images as you would any other book. If they are not good enough, then maybe that book is not right for you or your children. Trust me, there are now plenty of books out there with diverse characters who go on wonderful adventures or are written about in a beautiful way.

Now, as with everything, we do not want to take this to the extreme. I am not saying that you cannot have books which explain that some families have two mums, or what autism is, or why some people wear a hijab. But do review your books and make sure they feature representation and a brilliant story, not just education about diversity. After all, for children to love a book, the story needs to come first.

Good intentions or good inclusion?

We all know that there is variation in the quality and messaging in all areas of literature and education, so we need to look carefully at the messaging in books, particularly in the earlier years of primary school. Take this example of a fictional book which is based on the concepts of a real book used in some schools:

Once upon a time, in a bustling city of winding streets and towering palaces, there lived a kind-hearted girl named Aliyah. She dreamed of exploring faraway lands and discovering hidden treasures. But there was a problem – only boys were allowed to enter the Cave of Wonders, where the greatest treasures lay.

Determined to follow her dreams, Aliyah stumbled upon a mysterious lamp nestled in the heart of the marketplace. Rubbing it gently, she released a magical genie who granted her one wish. With a heart full of hope, Aliyah wished to become Ali, a brave young boy, so he could venture into the Cave of Wonders.

As Ali, he embarked on a thrilling adventure, accompanied by his faithful friend, the mischievous monkey, Abu. Together, they navigated treacherous deserts and faced daunting challenges, all to reach the fabled cave and uncover its secrets.

Inside the cave, Ali proved his worthiness by facing the trials with courage and integrity. In the end, he emerged victorious, clutching the lamp that held the power to change his destiny.

But, more important than the treasures he found, was the realisation that bravery and kindness know no gender. With the lamp's magic, Ali chose to remain true to himself, embracing both his dreams and his identity as Aliyah. And so, with the lamp's light guiding their way, Ali and Abu returned home, where they were celebrated as heroes, teaching everyone that true treasure lies within the courage to be yourself.

At first glance, this may seem like an interesting version of a story where the gender of the character has been flipped – a common tool in exploring alternative fairy tales. However, when we delve deeper into the story, some problematic messaging arises. With stories, we need to ask ourselves what messages are being given? What stereotypes are being reinforced? What is the purpose of the story? Take a moment to answer these three questions about this story.

The main problem with this story is that it conveys the idea that if Aliyah wants to succeed, she should transition to Ali, which is not a positive message to give to girls and is not what being transgender means. The use of stories like this may indicate that staff are trying to be inclusive, which is a wonderful thing, but that more training is needed for them to appreciate the nuances around such materials.

This is not to say that this story should not be used, but we need to comprehend the messaging around it. Are stereotypes being challenged? Are discussions around it age-appropriate? The answers to these questions can give us an insight into how sex and gender are discussed in the school and how we can develop the finer nuances of the topic.

It is usually out of good intentions that concepts are distilled down to enable children to understand them. However, this can create problems if stereotypes are reinforced and misconceptions are introduced. The number of books I see where gender is indicated by a girl wearing a bow is frustrating. If the only way we can explain a concept as complex as gender is through showing girls with bows in their hair, then we have to question whether those children are ready to grasp what we are talking about.

I am not saying that we should not discuss gender at all in the early years, but the focus should be on challenging stereotypes and allowing children to be themselves, so they feel free to explore their own identity when they are ready.

Building your bookshelves

When I began to investigate how inclusive the books in my own school were, it felt like a very daunting task. How would I know I was covering all aspects of diversity? What if I left a group out? Which aspects of diversity should be addressed through storybooks?

You already have a framework available that can help with this task: the protected characteristics. Using these as a starting point, I have distilled the characteristics into six key areas that resonate particularly in storybooks: diverse families, sex and challenging gender stereotypes, religion, visible disabilities, non-visible disabilities, and race. These categories provide a manageable and focused framework to guide the process and make this task more approachable.

1. Diverse families: Select books that showcase different family structures, such as single-parent families, same-sex parents, foster families, or extended families. Stories like these reflect the variety of home lives children experience.

2. Sex and challenging gender stereotypes: Look for books that portray boys and girls in non-traditional roles – for example, a story about a boy who loves ballet or a girl who builds robots – to encourage the children to explore their interests without the constraints of gender norms.

3. Religion: Search for books where characters of different faiths are part of the story without their religion being the sole focus – for example, a Muslim character who is simply a friend or a Jewish protagonist on a mystery-solving adventure – to make faith a natural part of life.

4. Visible disabilities: Ensure the representation of characters with physical disabilities as active participants in the story – for instance, a protagonist who uses a wheelchair might lead their team to victory in a school science competition.

5. Non-visible disabilities: Select books that sensitively portray characters with non-visible disabilities such as autism, ADHD, stammers, or mental health challenges. These stories can offer an insight into the experiences of others and reduce stigma.

6. Race: Prioritise books that feature racially diverse characters in a wide range of roles and narratives. These characters should

be depicted with depth and authenticity, celebrating their identities without making them the main focus of the story.

Before you begin to improve representation in your texts, take some time to create a list of the books you use already. You are looking for characters that are integral to the story, fully realised, and authentic. For example, when selecting books that feature characters from different racial or religious backgrounds, it is essential that their race or religion is not the sole focus of the narrative. A character who is Black, Muslim, or Jewish can be a hero, a friend, or an adventurer without the story needing to revolve around their identity. This approach usualises diversity and allows all children to see these characters as relatable and multifaceted. Do not include books with titles such as 'About Divali', as these are usually teaching texts, not representative texts.

In the early years, you may need to repeat this exercise each term, as you will go through many picture books during this time, and they should include a wide range of representation. Ensure that you include books read in story time and in your topics.

In Key Stage 2, you will use fewer books, so look across an entire year. Aim to include the books used in guided reading as well as your topics.

In secondary school, this survey is likely to be the focus of the English and humanities departments. Evaluate the entirety of a pupil's school life to identify what books they encounter.

In the Useful Resources at the back of this book, you can find a planning tool to help you review your current library and identify any gaps.

Once this exercise is complete, you will have a good idea of how inclusive and representative your books are. However, please do not think that every book needs to have minority representation; after all, White, straight, and able-bodied people exist in our society too. My favourite book to teach was Roald Dahl's *George's Marvellous Medicine*. This did not have any minority or under-represented diversity in it, but my classes loved the book and it inspired loads of amazing work. Sometimes, you might choose a book for its creativity, humour, or narrative strength, and it can still have a profound impact on pupils without explicitly addressing diversity.

Who are our role models?

When considering the role models that pupils learn about, I first want you to consider why we have role models in our curriculum. Role models provide a window into the past and help us to understand not only the societal situation but also the individual contributions and situations that people were living in at that time. In the present day, they can be used to inspire children and help them see their place in society. As no one lives in a family or community where every type of diversity is represented, books can also help usualise identities that pupils are unfamiliar with.

In Chapter 3, I asked you to consider your role models – who they are, where they come from, and what their characteristics are. If you identified a lack of diversity or a focus on international or historical role models, do not panic; you are definitely not on your own. Changing a curriculum to make it more inclusive takes time, but one of the first and most straightforward steps is to develop the inclusivity of the role models in our curriculum.

Consider the experience of a newly qualified teacher coming to your school. How would they know which role models they should be teaching, so they are included, but also that there is not overlap with other departments or year groups? How would they know whether there are gaps in the provision?

Depending on your curriculum you might consider one of these three methods of mapping your role models:

1. Adding to existing curriculum maps.

2. Creating a role models curriculum map.

3. Building a resource bank of role models.

If you already have curriculum maps in place, adding role models can be a way of ensuring that you have representative role models across the school without creating another bit of paperwork. Consider tagging them with how they contribute to the diversity of the curriculum, so you are ensuring a wide range of representation. This method ensures that role models are seen as part of the curriculum, but it can be more challenging to consider your role models as a whole and ensure coverage and progression.

Creating a separate document which outlines the role models and their purpose in the curriculum for each year group and topic has the benefit of making coverage and progression easier to track. However, it can also become just another document that isn't used or makes planning more complicated.

If your curriculum is not fixed each year, or if you would prefer to allow staff to choose role models based on the cohort and the curriculum at that time, a bank of role models can provide teachers with the resources they need to include role models where appropriate. This can be empowering, but you will need to have regular discussions with staff to ensure that role models are not being repeated and there is coverage across all the protected characteristics.

As with all major curriculum development, realistically role models work is only going to succeed if a large number of staff are collaborating. Not only does this spread the workload, but it also ensures that the curriculum change is achieved *with* them and not *to* them. You also get the benefit of local knowledge; many of our staff have grown up in the area and may know ex-pupils or local figures who can be used as role models.

In primary school, it is much easier for the whole staff to be involved – and I would also advise you to invite support staff and even governors and parents. The more people you include in this process, the more experience you bring to the task, and the greater the likelihood that you will identify a range of role models that you may never have heard of before.

In secondary school, departments can work together to create role model maps. Even with department working, I would recommend that you gather in the same rooms or near each other, as teams will need expertise from outside their immediate area for some role models.

Where do we learn about role models?

The curriculum plays a powerful role in shaping how pupils see themselves, others, and their place in the world. However, I often find that schools teach pupils about events and role models who feel distant or disconnected from their lives; I have been guilty of this too. These are figures from far-off lands, long-past eras, or experiences so far removed from their own that pupils struggle to find any relevance or meaning in them. While it is crucial to celebrate significant historical figures and global trail-blazers, we also need to reflect on whether they genuinely resonate with the pupils in our classrooms.

Take Martin Luther King Jr as an example. Most adults and older pupils will recognise his name and know about his role in the civil rights movement. However, focusing so heavily on King's story can unintentionally give the impression that racism was, and is, only a problem in the United States. Why do we not place equal emphasis on British figures who fought against racial injustice? Why is there so little focus on people like Olive Morris or Darcus Howe or events such as the Bristol bus boycott? I believe this is because the curriculum has been shaped by historical and cultural biases that spotlight the achievements of other nations while neglecting struggles and successes closer to home. This approach not only distances pupils from the subject but also denies them the chance to see how racism has been, and continues to be, tackled in their own country.

We also need to ask whether pupils are ready to engage with the complexity of the figures and events we introduce. For example, many primary schools teach their pupils about Alan Turing as a pioneer of computing, but they often leave out the discrimination he faced as a gay man in post-war Britain. This simplifies his life to a story of technological innovation, ignoring the personal and societal challenges that shaped his legacy. Similarly, primary age children are sometimes taught about the Stonewall riots, but they lack the understanding to grasp its implications as a catalyst for the modern LGBTQ+ rights movement. By teaching children about these people and events too early, we risk reducing their significance and missing the opportunity to have meaningful, age-appropriate discussions about identity, oppression, and activism.

During a visit to Jubilee Park Primary School in South Wales, I saw an approach that helps pupils to connect more meaningfully with the people and events they learn about. The school has adapted Valerie Hannon and Amelia Peterson's levels of thriving framework to support their curriculum design. They adopt the following four layers to decide when and how to introduce aspects of the curriculum: intrapersonal, interpersonal, societal, and global.[3] In the early years, the focus is on the *intrapersonal* level – pupils learn about their immediate family and close circles. In Key Stage 1, the *interpersonal* layer introduces role models from the local area and community. In Years 3 and 4, the focus shifts to *societal* connections, such as figures and events from Wales. By Years 5 and 6, pupils are ready to explore *global* influences across the UK and beyond. For LGBTQ+ inclusion, this might start with discussing diverse family structures in the early years, move to learning about local LGBTQ+ activists or allies in Key Stage 1, and then progress to national figures in early Key Stage 2 and the impact of inclusion as the pupils reach upper Key Stage 2. This framework helps to gradually build pupils' understanding, making sure the role models are relatable and age-appropriate.

This framework is not just helpful for primary schools; it can be incredibly valuable for secondary schools too. At this stage, pupils are developing a deeper understanding of complex issues and forming their own perspectives on the world. By using the intrapersonal, interpersonal, societal, and global layers as a focus, you can ensure that the role models and events you teach resonate with their experiences while also expanding their horizons. For example, in a history unit about civil rights, you might begin with local figures who fought for equality in your region before exploring national movements and then connecting these to global struggles. In PSHE, you could use the framework to introduce LGBTQ+ inclusion, starting with stories of local activists, then discussing national policies like the Equality Act, and finally addressing international contexts such as the global fight for marriage equality. This approach not only helps pupils to see the relevance of what

---

3   V. Hannon and A. Peterson, *Thrive: The Purpose of Schools in a Changing World* (Cambridge: Cambridge University Press, 2021), p. 37.

they are learning but also encourages them to consider their place within these broader narratives.

Primary school role model framework

Focus level	People	Events	Places
Intrapersonal	Immediate family or close circles	Birthdays or personal achievements	Home or local area
Interpersonal	Local community leaders or allies	Community festivals or local activism	Local landmarks or spaces
Societal	National figures	Regional movements or historic events	Regional landmarks
Global	International trail-blazers	World Pride or global historical events	Global cities or historic sites

Secondary school role model framework

Focus level	People	Events	Places
Intrapersonal	Immediate family or personal influences	Personal milestones or achievements	Local community spaces or home
Interpersonal	Local leaders, activists, or historical figures	Community movements or notable local events	Towns or regions with local significance

Focus level	People	Events	Places
Societal	National figures shaping society (e.g. writers, politicians)	National movements or legislative changes	Key national locations (e.g. London, Edinburgh)
Global	International leaders or influencers	Global movements, conflicts, or collaborations	Global cities or historically significant locations

Blank versions of these tables can be found in the Useful Resources section. This is a practical tool to reflect on the role models, events, and places that are already part of your curriculum and to spot any patterns or gaps. For example, does your curriculum focus heavily on global figures while overlooking local contributions? It is also great for planning future topics. By systematically working through the four layers, you can ensure that pupils are introduced to relatable, age-appropriate role models that gradually expand their worldview.

This might not be the right approach for every school, but it is worth considering how relatable your role models are, particularly at Key Stage 2 and in secondary school. It is so easy to bypass local and regional influences in favour of global figures and events, meaning that pupils miss the chance to connect with the people, places, and events that reflect their own communities and identities. Recognising local and regional role models is a crucial step in making the curriculum both meaningful and inspiring for every child.

What do our role models tell us?

In this chapter, you have carefully considered who and what you have learned about, and how they relate to your pupils. The role models and stories we include in our curriculum send powerful messages to pupils about how their identities are valued and how the world around them is shaped. Every school's community is unique and so, as educators, we have a dual responsibility: to ensure that every young person feels seen and has a sense of belonging, while also exposing them to the broader world beyond their immediate environment.

When selecting role models to improve diversity and representation, it is essential to consider the meaning they hold for pupils. In the early years, when children might explore topics like 'people who help us', there are prime opportunities to challenge stereotypes. Representation must be intentional and relatable – for example, using real people from the local community, such as parents or community members, instead of animated or cartoon characters ensures authenticity. Cartoons often perpetuate stereotypes and lack the personal connection children need to make meaningful associations. Inviting families to contribute photographs can make role models more tangible and reflective of the pupils' own environments.

As pupils progress through school, their understanding of the world widens, but role models still need a personal connection to resonate. Even in secondary school, learning about someone who attended the same school or grew up locally can have a greater impact than focusing solely on distant or unrelatable figures. This balance helps pupils to connect with the stories they hear, making the curriculum more relevant and inspiring.

Representation must also challenge stereotypes in a thoughtful and balanced way. For instance, when discussing disability, many schools default to showcasing Paralympians. These individuals are extraordinary role models, and their achievements should be celebrated. However, if this is the only representation of disability, it may unintentionally create the impression that all disabled people must excel in sports to be recognised. Learning about local people with disabilities and sharing their everyday lives and contributions can provide a more rounded and realistic understanding of inclusion.

A similar challenge exists when teaching about LGBTQ+ inclusion. Alan Turing is a common figure in primary school curricula, and his contributions to history are remarkable. However, his story also carries themes of persecution and tragedy. If the majority of LGBTQ+ role models share narratives of adversity or sad endings, what messages are being given? While lessons should be designed to acknowledge struggle and foster empathy, the curriculum must balance this with positive and life-affirming stories. LGBTQ+ pupils need to see role models who reflect joy, success, and acceptance, ensuring that their identities are not solely associated with adversity.

By carefully selecting role models, ensuring their age-appropriateness, and balancing positive and negative narratives, we can create a curriculum that inspires, challenges stereotypes, and helps every child to feel seen. This is not just about representation; it is about shaping a more inclusive and empathetic society where everyone feels a sense of belonging.

Challenging stereotypes

Ask any early years teacher and most would agree that in nursery children wear whatever they want, but over the next two years they become more aware of gendered clothing, and their views on what they 'should' wear narrows.

Our society is very gendered and often reinforces harmful conventions; you only have to walk into some toy shops to see the pink aisle and the blue (or combat) aisle. It is our responsibility as educators to tackle these cultural restrictions and help our children and young people to be who they want to be. Stereotypes are deeply ingrained in us for a very good reason. In evolutionary terms, they allow us to quickly make decisions and assess threats. But in the modern world, they often manifest as bias and prejudice against minority or under-represented groups and to those different from us. As schools, we cannot prevent societal stereotypes in their entirety, but we can contribute to challenging them and giving our pupils a more balanced view of the world.

Images have great power. I am not saying that you can never show an image of a male doctor, a female hairdresser, a family with a mum and dad, or a woman doing housework, but if they represent the prevailing imagery we use, particularly in primary schools, we are reinforcing the views that certain roles belong to certain people and that families look a specific way. Study the images in your books together as a staff and think about what they are telling your children about people in our society. Are you seeing traditional roles being challenged? You do not need to make a lesson out of this, and each image you show does not have to come with a lecture about smashing stereotypes; sometimes seeing the image is enough. If you do this right, over time, the subliminal message will get through that we are all capable of chasing our dreams and everyone is capable of great things (and not great things).

As we saw with our role models earlier, we need to ensure that LGBTQ+ role models in particular are rounded and have a variety of perspectives: not all gay men are camp or flamboyant, not all lesbians are masculine, not all LGBTQ+ people were imprisoned or castrated, and so on. This is especially important with literature and film: again, what images are you presenting to your pupils? This is not to say that we can never show a camp gay character, but are we showing a range of gay men who are not camp?

This is also an opportunity to challenge some of the stereotypes around being transgender and non-binary. All too often, I see schools using popstars or social media influencers to explain these concepts to their pupils. While they will be recognisable to many young people, these celebrities have a carefully crafted image that is often about gaining attention and notoriety, which is a far cry from the everyday life of transgender and non-binary people. They are often perceived as attention-seeking or as only ever talking about their gender identity. Selecting role models from your community or using the resources available online from organisations such as Diversity Role Models,[4] you can make sure that you present role models who are far closer to the experiences of your pupils. Ultimately, most gender-divergent people just want to get on with their lives, not garner lots of attention.

Gay woodwork

When you begin to talk about embedding diversity in your school, certain subjects will naturally lend themselves to exploring different identities, histories, and perspectives. In history, you can examine how LGBTQ+ people and other marginalised groups have

---

4   See www.diversityrolemodels.org.

been treated over time, ensuring that you are not just telling a dominant narrative but rather a broad and inclusive one. In English, you have a rich opportunity to introduce diverse texts, showcasing authors and characters from different backgrounds, identities, and experiences. These subjects provide clear and direct avenues for discussing diversity, but what about those subjects where representation is less obvious?

Subjects such as IT, design and technology, and even maths do not always seem to have an immediate link to diversity and inclusion. There are fewer explicit discussions about identity in these areas, and traditional teaching in these subjects has often been focused on skills and processes rather than social perspectives. However, that does not mean that diversity is irrelevant in these spaces – it just means that the approach must be different.

One of the most practical ways to introduce diversity into these subjects is by considering who is engaging with them. Looking at the demographics of pupils taking certain courses can reveal entrenched stereotypes. How many boys are taking textiles? How many girls are in electronics? Are non-binary pupils feeling comfortable in any of these traditionally gendered spaces? Addressing these disparities is key to ensuring that all pupils feel encouraged to explore all areas of learning.

Another way to embed diversity is by inviting diverse role models and visitors into schools to challenge entrenched stereotypes. Assemblies and guest speaker sessions can provide powerful opportunities for pupils to hear from individuals with different backgrounds and experiences, showcasing the breadth of talent in all fields. Bringing in LGBTQ+ professionals, female engineers, or disabled technologists can broaden perspectives and encourage pupils to consider paths they may not have previously seen as options. By making these role models visible, schools can actively work against narrow ideas of who 'belongs' in certain careers and foster a more inclusive environment.

In subjects where representation alone may not be enough, diversity can be integrated by challenging stereotypes directly. This includes making sure that boys feel just as welcome in food technology as they do in woodwork and ensuring that girls are encouraged to pursue engineering. Schools can rethink the language used when introducing these subjects, avoiding gendered assumptions about who might excel in them. Additionally, class-room activities can be designed to reflect a range of cultural influences – whether through studying the impact of global design or ensuring that examples used in coding and programming reflect diverse contexts.

However, addressing pupil perceptions is only part of the battle; parental attitudes can also be a significant barrier. Many parents still hold outdated beliefs about which subjects are 'suitable' for their children based on gender or other factors. Schools should be proactive in engaging with families to challenge these ideas. This could involve highlighting diverse role models in parent communications, ensuring that careers advice does not reinforce traditional pathways, and directly addressing gender stereotypes during parents' evenings or information sessions.

Ultimately, ensuring diversity in every subject is about more than just representation – it is about actively challenging barriers that prevent all pupils from feeling that they belong. Whether through role models, curriculum choices, or addressing entrenched stereotypes, every subject has the potential to be inclusive without having gay woodwork.

Building a curriculum for all

Representation in schools is not just a nice-to-have; it is essential. When you choose books that reflect a range of experiences, you are giving your pupils the chance to see themselves and others in new and inspiring ways. It is about showing them what is possible and opening their eyes to the richness of the world around them.

By bringing in local role models, you can make success feel real and achievable for your pupils. And when you challenge stereotypes – whether in the stories you share, the lessons you teach, or the conversations you have – you are actively breaking down barriers and showing young people that they do not have to fit into a box to succeed.

Even the visuals around your classroom or school matter more than you might think. Posters, displays, and the images you use in lessons send powerful messages. When those messages are inclusive, they tell every child, 'You belong here, just as you are.'

It might feel like a lot to get right, but every small step you take towards better representation makes a difference. The more you commit to this, the more you will see the impact in your pupils – their confidence, their sense of self, their belief that they can do anything. So, keep pushing for that change. Your efforts can shape futures in ways you might not even realise.

Chapter 7

All Aboard the LGBTQ+ Express

· ·

I'm not sure I can honestly say that I always wanted to be a parent. Certainly, a part of this was the narrative from my formative years where you had to be in a straight relationship to have a family. Until this time, there was very little conversation about same-sex couples having children. But during my early 30s, when all my friends began having children, I realised that I did want a child and that I could be a good dad to a child who needed me.

In 2013, we started the adoption process and adopted our son when he was 2 years old. Being an adoptive parent means that you get lots of training on trauma and life story work but not a single thing about changing nappies. Believe me when I say that the first couple of changes were not successful! But the joy of becoming a parent was worth all the challenging moments.

At the time, I never really thought about the monumental change of being allowed to become same-sex parents. After all, it was only 11 years before we started the process that same-sex parents were allowed to adopt legally in the UK. Everyone else always seemed to be happier about this milestone than I was. I still wonder why: did I not want to consider myself as a trail-blazer? Was I still dealing with the internalised homophobia I had battled since I came out?

Books are really important in our house. Our son has always loved bedtime, and stories are a core part of the routine. One of the first books he chose from the library was *Baking with Dad* by Aurora Cacciapuoti.[1] Although we didn't realise until we got the book home, the daughter and father are actually making a cake for another man. It is not part of the story and

---

1 A. Cacciapuoti, *Baking with Dad* (London: Child's Play International, 2016).

it is not mentioned apart from the pictures; it is left open for the reader to decide whether it is two dads or a relative. I loved this way of doing it. Although there are many wonderful books that teach children about same-sex parents, I often felt that they put the representation before the story, so we avoided them. But *Baking with Dad* became a staple in our house, and we both know the words off by heart.

I was reading to my son one night when he was about 7 years old – the wonderful *Ned and the Lonely Fisherman* by Ian Eagleton.[2] In this story, a merman called Ned meets a lonely fisherman. Now, without too many spoilers, this is the beginning of a beautiful story. Again, when I got the book, I didn't know it had an LGBTQ+ theme, but it didn't really matter as the story and artwork are beautiful.

It started me thinking about my son's favourite books. Apart from those which are gross or downright hilarious, his favourites have one thing in common: two dads. I asked him what other books he had read in school that featured two dads, and he replied, 'None.' It was a moment of awakening. At first, I was angry at his school, until I began to reflect on my own practice and my own education. How many times had I read stories with same-sex parents? How many times had I avoided the truth about people in history because they were rumoured to be gay or bisexual (for example, Alexander the Great, Oscar Wilde, and Virginia Woolf)?

This was the start of my journey to realising that our education system can sometimes give a narrow view of the world. When details about individuals are ignored or even changed to suit a dated narrative, it creates a world that does not represent our own. I spent the next few months learning about my own culture, leading to the realisation that just because I was a gay man, it did not mean that I instinctively knew what an inclusive curriculum looked like. Since then, I have been on a continuing journey: getting to know books with inclusive characters, learning about age-appropriateness in this area, and, most importantly, accepting how restricted a world I had previously provided for my pupils. But what has shocked me the most throughout this process has been not my own need

---

2   I. Eagleton, *Ned and the Lonely Fisherman* (Leamington Spa: Owlet Press, 1991).

to learn more but grasping that some people are resistant or even opposed to these changes.

....

The heteronormative culture that envelops our lives is based on the idea that ideas such as aromanticism or polyamory are somehow incongruous with the ideals of heterosexuality or traditional monogamy that exclude identities such as demisexuality or gender fluidity.

Now, if you read the paragraph above and felt a bit lost, you are not alone (unless you have been doing a lot of reading on the subject since Chapter 1; I made it up, by the way). I intentionally chose this example to highlight how overwhelming discussions around gender and sexuality can feel for some people. The language surrounding these topics is as fluid as gender and sexuality themselves, and it can be a daunting task to keep up. When approaching the shift to greater inclusivity, we need to be considerate that not everyone will be as confident or as motivated as we are.

People often bring preconceived ideas to the table about what others know or believe on these topics, so it is crucial to approach this work with an open mind and limit any biases as much as possible. It can be difficult to assess where your staff stand on LGBTQ+ issues, as it requires openness and honesty in an area where many people feel anxious or unsure, so assume that there are people who will be resistant to these changes for reasons that are very valid for them.

In this chapter, I want you to think about how you will approach changes to your policies, procedures, and curriculum. If you are passionate about LGBTQ+ inclusion, it can be easy to want to see progress quickly. However, rushing or pushing too hard can alienate the very people you need to bring on board. It is also tempting to dismiss those who are not directly engaged in DEIB work – but remember, bringing the most resistant people along with you will make the process of change more sustainable and effective in the long term. Starting with the basics, planning, and pacing yourself are key to making meaningful progress in fostering an inclusive environment.

Be prepared

I do not want to tell you what you already know, but I will share some methods for planning approaches that have worked for me, especially when dealing with something as complex as developing diversity and inclusion.

When thinking about designing your approach to training, development, and change management, it can help to plan it out in a table like the one on page 131, considering all the areas that we have discussed.

Map the activities using the impact/effort matrix in Chapter 3, considering the best order and how long they will take. Be realistic about what you can achieve, and also try to make sure that things occur in the right order. It is pointless delivering training on anti-bullying, for example, if you have not nailed down your policies and procedures. I love using a long roll of paper and sticky notes for this.

You may also want to consider adding in other school improvement changes on the same document. After all, work to improve inclusion should not happen in isolation from the rest of school development. For instance, if you are looking at books, this needs to align closely with your literacy action plan; if you are looking at role models, every subject action plan should reflect these steps; and if you are going to involve the governing body or trust, this needs to be factored into their own agenda. By integrating all your plans together, it is far less likely that this essential work will be forgotten about and pushed out by more important tasks.

Nothing irritates me more than insisting that change must fit within one academic year. The reality is that this change will take place over several years, and you will have to consider when you will revisit these topics, especially with new staff.

	Autumn term	Winter term	Spring term	Summer term
Strong foundations (vision)	School health check Developing a vision statement			Review of health check Revisit vision statement
Policy	Update policies			
Pastoral		Staff training on tackling bullying and supporting pupils		
Provision			Staff training on an inclusive curriculum	
Representation and role models			Map and develop role models across the curriculum	
Community	Feedback from stakeholders on inclusion	Governor training on anti-bullying and inclusion	Parent–teacher association (PTA) group to find inclusive books for the library	Community event

LGBTQ+ 101

Once you are ready to commence the first inclusivity training session with staff, listen to Lewis Carroll and 'Begin at the beginning'. When delivering training, too often we jump in to what we are going to do and forget about the why. In Simon Sinek style, you are going to start with why this work is important.[3] If people are not invested in this exercise, then why would they care? We have all been in that training session where we have no idea how it relates to us, and instead spend our time planning our next holiday, coming up with plans for dinner, or checking our emails.

You need to get members of staff on board, so that when you do start to introduce changes, they are right there with you. As we saw in the Introduction, not creating an inclusive environment for LGBTQ+ pupils has real-life mental-health implications. As hard as it may be, demonstrating and talking to staff about the statistics surrounding bullying and its long-term impacts are essential in making sure that everyone understands the importance of DEIB work. Sharing the data around the impact of not creating an inclusive environment can be difficult for some people to hear, but it can put into the forefront the urgency of this work.

One of the most effective ways for staff to see that inclusion has real-life impact is to hear from real people. When I begin my training, I talk about my childhood and the effect of my school's neglect of inclusivity on me and my life. It is very difficult to argue with someone's experience, especially when they are right in front of you. You might have staff confident enough to talk about their experiences to the rest of the school community, but we should not coerce or pressure anyone into this. Reflecting on negative school experiences can be very triggering for some; I still find it challenging, even after having done it dozens of times. If you do not have someone in school who is willing to speak out, you might consider inviting in a visitor or using one of the many videos that are available for free online. There is a reason that using real people works with pupils, and it works with staff too.

---

3 S. Sinek, *Start with Why: How Great Leaders Inspire Everyone to Take Action* (New York: Penguin, 2009).

However, you need to be cautious about creating a solely negative view of LGBTQ+ inclusion. If you only focus on the depressing statistics and harmful impacts, staff could be disillusioned before you even begin. Ensure that when you are introducing the reasons for DEIB, you also talk about the positives of this work – that pupils will feel safe, seen, and supported. Whether it is enjoying new books with inclusive characters, learning about interesting role models, or taking the opportunity to develop the curriculum, this should be a process that you and your staff enjoy.

Please do not plan to do all this work in a single training session. Not only will that be far too brief, but people need time to change their attitudes and for new information to sink in. The topics set out in the table above might take place over a year or even several. It is far better to take your time and get this right than waste your time with a virtue-signalling training session that has no impact.

Starting with LGBTQ+ vocabulary

As we saw in Chapter 1, having a common understanding of language and concepts is important for conversations about inclusion to happen.

When you are ready to develop staff knowledge of vocabulary, view this activity in the same way that you would pupil learning. Listing off vocabulary and their definitions will limit engagement from the participants. There are far more creative ways of doing this, such as:

+ An online quiz where people match up definitions with words. After each question, discuss what the words mean and why certain answers are correct and incorrect. (This is my personal favourite which I use in my training sessions.)

+ Play bingo where you call out definitions and the staff have to match to the words on their card. When someone calls 'Bingo!' talk through their answers with the group.

+ Give mixed-up words and definitions to each table and ask the groups to unscramble them. How quickly can each table reorder them?

Throw in a few rubbish prizes, and I guarantee that the staff will be on side!

Some of these ideas might seem a bit silly (who does not like a bit of silliness?), but many people are genuinely anxious about vocabulary, so wherever possible we need to help them relax. Using games and practical activities avoids the boredom of a presentation but also makes the topic more interesting.

Changing hearts and minds

Unfortunately, you may be in a situation in your school where – even after sharing the statistics, the reason for going on this journey, and hearing real-life stories – there may still be some members of staff who are resistant to the work or do not see it as their responsibility. This can be for a myriad of reasons, but in my experience the main ones are religious beliefs, personal experiences (or lack of), and exposure to misinformation.

I have many friends who are LGBTQ+ and from many different faiths. What becomes clear when you talk to most people of faith is that religion does not spread hate, people do. What I am going to address here comes from conversations with individuals with various belief systems but all with common messages. The length of most religious texts and the number of translations means you are always going to be able to find a passage that justifies almost any belief or behaviour. However, when we come to apply these precepts in a modern context, they are often difficult to use literally. Even if we do take passages literally, we cannot forget that the main tenets of all the major religions are based on love, respect, and supporting one another. Why would this be different for certain communities?

Moreover, as a friend who runs a Church in Wales school once told me, 'God never says that He will love anyone less than anyone else.' Although religion is a protected characteristic in many countries, and everyone is entitled to their own beliefs, this does not give them the right to discriminate. This is where your school vision and values are vital. As members of the school community, everyone should be on board with these principles, or you will not create an environment where every pupil is safe, seen, and supported. Senior leaders should respect religious views, but you need to make clear that discrimination of any sort does not have a place in your school.

Everyone has their own personal beliefs and experiences that change over time. I grew up in a place that was very White, focused almost exclusively on rugby (which only boys played), and where men certainly did not talk about mental health. This environment gave me values and beliefs that shaped how I viewed the world. It can be very challenging to change our views, and they will not change overnight. Throughout this process, there will be members of staff whose core beliefs are being challenged. To expect them to change instantly is unrealistic, and to pillory people who are going through the process of change might entrench them in their views and have the opposite effect.

First, these individuals need time to process new information, so they can make incremental changes. Next, they need regular training on why DEIB work is necessary. This could be in the form of short refresher sessions as part of your own staff meeting schedule. Alternatively, there are many online training platforms that offer short training offerings. The key with this training is that it must be purpose driven and make clear *why* LGBTQ+ inclusion is important rather than *what* needs to change in schools.

Finally, do not avoid conversations about this topic. You need to be direct that inclusion work aligns with the values of the school and will be proceeding (and just how wonderful that is). By creating a longer term vision, we can give these individuals the chance to grow and learn. However, while we should appreciate that some people grow up in certain environments and have certain beliefs, this cannot be used as an excuse for prejudice. Even those people who are learning should be moving along with the changes in the school, even if they do not quite understand why, yet.

The other main group I come across in schools who do not support inclusion work have been exposed to misinformation, usually on social media. There is a plethora of false information about LGBTQ+ inclusion and RSE out there, and I have certainly seen an increase in both the quantity and extremism of this material. Often presented as a concern for young people, the posts generally twist real-life events or announcements to suggest that there are behaviours going on in schools that have no bearing on reality.

The primary way to combat false information is through education and transparency. Whether they are teachers, support staff, parents, governors, or any other stakeholders, if we educate people on why we are doing this work and are completely transparent about the resources and activities we are using, then we can show the misinformation for what it truly is. Everyone should have access to your policies, curriculum statements, and safeguarding procedures via your website. Plus, any parent should be able to see any curriculum resources, if requested. However, to avoid misunderstandings, I would advise you to invite parents in to view them, so that you can explain the full context of the resource, rather than sending it out when it could be misinterpreted.

It can be easy to judge people who have views on inclusion that differ from our own, but we must remember that everyone is on a journey. While there is never an excuse for prejudice, change takes time. The main thing we need to ask people to do is to learn. For some, that learning will happen at once or in a single training session. For others, it may take them months or years to really shift their beliefs. Although it is difficult, I would ask you to give these individuals the time they need, because if you want long-term change, you need to recognise that people progress in their own time and have different amounts of information to learn and unlearn.

The power and purpose of symbols

Although the whole point of this book is about avoiding virtue signalling, when symbols like rainbow lanyards, badges, and pronouns in email signatures occur in combination with wider institutional changes, they can play a powerful role in creating a more inclusive school environment. These signs send a clear message of support and solidarity, signalling to pupils, staff, and families that LGBTQ+ inclusion matters. However, their effectiveness depends on how they are used and understood within the school community.

Symbols should be deployed with intention and purpose, not as superficial gestures. For example, wearing a rainbow lanyard or displaying a Pride badge means that you are identifying yourself as an ally or a safe person to talk to. This is a meaningful commitment, not just a fashion statement. Staff need to understand what these symbols represent and be prepared to back them up with action, whether that is offering support to a pupil or confidently challenging inappropriate behaviour. Without this foundation, symbols risk becoming hollow or performative.

It is also vital to ensure that you do not thrust the use of these symbols on staff. Not everyone may feel comfortable or ready to wear a visible sign of allyship, and that is okay. Forcing participation can lead to resentment or discomfort and undermine the authenticity of the message. Instead, create opportunities for staff to learn about the purpose behind these symbols and choose whether to adopt them. This choice is important because true allyship comes from a place of understanding and willingness, not obligation.

Similarly, adding pronouns to email signatures is a simple but impactful way to usualise conversations about gender identity. For some, it is a powerful tool for demonstrating inclusivity and breaking down assumptions about gender. However, it is crucial that this, too, remains a personal choice. People should feel empowered to add pronouns if they wish, but they should also understand why this action matters. Providing staff with the context is key. Explain that including pronouns can help to create a more inclusive environment for transgender and non-binary individuals by reducing the likelihood of misgendering and showing respect for everyone's identities. At the same time, acknowledge that some people may need time to feel comfortable with this practice. Similarly, staff should not be required to provide their pronouns at the beginning of meetings, but they should feel confident to do so if this is important to them.

When symbols like lanyards, badges, and pronouns are used with purpose and backed up with genuine understanding, they can be very powerful. By ensuring they are adopted thoughtfully and voluntarily, your school can send a strong, authentic message of support to everyone in the community.

Sustaining change

Once you have begun your journey towards improving LGBTQ+ inclusion, the key to success is keeping that momentum going. Change does not happen overnight, and it certainly does not stop after an initial push. To create lasting impact, you need to sustain the efforts you have started. In the next section, we will focus on how you can maintain momentum, celebrate progress, and keep the train on track.

Monitoring progress and celebrating small wins

To ensure you are heading in the right direction, it is essential to track your progress. Take a step back and reflect on the strategies you have put in place. Collect feedback through surveys, conversations, and observations. Have your initial goals been met? Are pupils, staff, and parents engaging in the process? What is working well? Where do you still need to make adjustments?

Celebrating wins is equally important. Big or small, it is vital to acknowledge and celebrate achievements along the way. Whether it is an increase in LGBTQ+ pupils feeling safe to express themselves or a teacher reporting more inclusive classroom practices, these milestones are significant. Recognition could come in many forms: shout-outs in staff meetings, recognition in school assemblies, or even something as simple as a thank-you card. Acknowledging progress keeps people motivated and helps everyone feel like they are part of something meaningful. Do not just collect feedback – use it. If something is not working as planned, tweak your approach. This is about finding out what works for your school community and continuing to evolve.

Providing ongoing support for staff and pupils

Sustaining change means ensuring everyone feels supported throughout the journey, both staff and pupils. You have started the work, but now it is about building a culture where LGBTQ+ inclusion is part of everyday life.

For staff, regular training and professional development are crucial to help them feel equipped and confident in their roles as LGBTQ+ allies. Ensure that training is varied and ongoing, not a one-off session. Staff meetings, workshops, or even informal discussions can keep inclusion at the forefront of everyone's minds. Offering resources, like reading materials, online courses, or opportunities to connect with LGBTQ+ organisations, can help to sustain engagement.

For pupils, make sure they continue to have access to the support they need. Peer-led LGBTQ+ groups or mentorship schemes can provide lasting support and create spaces for them to express themselves. Remember, pupils often thrive when they know they are not alone, so encourage them to share their experiences and feed back about school culture.

Adjusting strategies based on feedback

While you will be celebrating your wins, you will also encounter challenges along the way. Resistance from some staff or pupils may not fade immediately. The key is to stay flexible and adjust your strategies as you go. As you receive feedback, adapt to better meet the needs of your community.

Be proactive, not reactive. Instead of waiting for problems to become crises, anticipate problems. Check in regularly with staff and pupils to gauge how things are going. What barriers are emerging? Do you need to adjust your policies or support systems to address those challenges? Adjust your approach to resistance. Resistance does not mean failure. If staff members continue to be resistant, dig a little deeper. Is the issue rooted in a lack of understanding? Does the person need more time? Are there personal biases to overcome? Approach these situations with patience and empathy, keeping in mind that everyone's journey towards inclusion looks different.

Ensuring leadership commitment

Sustaining momentum requires ongoing support from leadership. It is one thing for a few staff members to be champions of LGBTQ+ inclusion, but it is another for that support to come from the top down.

Ensure that your school's leadership team are fully on board with the journey. Their commitment is crucial in setting the tone and ensuring that policies and practices are fully supported across the school. Regularly check in with them to ensure that LGBTQ+ inclusion remains a priority and that they are taking an active role in fostering this culture.

Encourage leaders to create a long-term vision for LGBTQ+ inclusion, looking beyond just your current efforts. What will your school look like in three or five years' time in terms of inclusion? How can you continue to move forward without losing sight of the progress already made?

Reflecting on the journey so far

Do not forget to take time to reflect. It is easy to get caught up in the next step, the next goal, or the next challenge. Pausing to acknowledge how far you have come can be a powerful motivator for you and your team. Reflect on the journey in a way that reminds everyone of the bigger picture.

Use milestones to remind the whole school why it matters. Whether it is a major change like revising the curriculum or a simple success like a staff member becoming more comfortable using inclusive language, celebrate those moments. These victories are proof that your efforts are making a difference.

Evaluating change

It can be tempting to think that there is an end to this journey and that you will evaluate when you get there. But the reality is that this is an ongoing process. Consider repeating the surveys each year or including the questions in a wider survey, so that you can continually update the picture of where your school and community are.

The key is to remain focused on your long-term goals and to recognise that even when things feel slow, you are making a difference and moving towards a culture where every person – no matter their sexual orientation or gender identity – feels safe, seen, and supported.

So, as you move forward, stay on the track. The destination may be a long way off, but you have already made incredible strides. Let us keep the train rolling.

Chapter 8

It Takes a Village: Working with the Community

By 2021, I had been teaching for about 14 years and had always been made to feel welcome for who I was. Between gifts for my adoption, my partner at the time volunteering at my school, and never having to hide the fact that I had a boyfriend, it had never occurred to me that some people weren't accepting of my identity. I suppose I was living in a protective bubble, so I was naive to the homophobia that still existed in society. I also had a very limited social-media presence and so didn't realise how vile online spaces could be for LGBTQ+ people.

After three years of being a deputy head, a new pupil in my class refused to come to school. Upon investigation, it transpired that he felt that a man adopting a child with another man was unnatural. It was clear from the pupil's language that they were not his own words, but those of his parents. Despite several meetings to discuss the issue, the pupil ended up missing a large proportion of the term, missing out on learning, social contact, and falling even further behind his peers. It was a challenging time as my entire focus was getting him back to school, and I felt tremendously guilty. Luckily, my head teacher and governing body were very supportive and refused to compromise on the values of the school. We were a very inclusive school, which meant that the expectation of being inclusive also extended to the children and parents. Eventually, due to an intervention by the attendance and well-being service, the child returned to school.

Within several weeks he was thriving, and we developed a really positive pupil–teacher relationship. Many of the misconceptions he had received were challenged, and this pupil actually met my son and they got on incredibly well. I am a true believer that most prejudice in our world comes from a lack of understanding due to misinformation or a lack of experience, and by remaining positive and being seen we can make the world a more accepting place.

It was at this point that I realised we still had a lot of work to do in society, and that many schools and local authorities just weren't doing enough, especially when engaging with parents and communities. So, I took the plunge, and in January 2023 I left teaching to set up what would become More Than Flags and Rainbows and eventually write this book.

. . . .

So far, I have talked almost exclusively from within the school grounds and buildings. But if inclusion is to be truly successful, then we need to look outside the gates. Not only must you communicate well with parents, families, and the community, but the most successful schools collaborate with their community rather than keeping them at arm's length.

It is important to explore how best to work with your community because these aspects can be the most challenging areas of diversity and inclusion – but also the most wonderful and celebratory. Whether it is inviting families into school, holding a Pride event, or just keeping parents clearly informed, being confident about sharing what you are doing with the community shows that you have belief in what you do and know exactly why you are doing it.

Compared to the content of earlier chapters, community working is the area that I believe is most bespoke to each school. Please do not look at the school down the road which is hosting a Pride event and feel that you have to do the same. Every school and every community is different, and you must do what is right for your pupils, staff, families, and community.

In this chapter, we will consider what takes place outside of school, including events you can hold, social-media reactions, and whether you should apply for awards to recognise your inclusion efforts. After all, it takes a village.

Working with parents

I would love to tell you that all parents will be on board and supportive from the start. While most will be, there will be a minority who are unhappy with the introduction or development of LGBTQ+ inclusion. The reasons behind this are complex but originate from many places including online misinformation, personal experiences at school, personal experiences with LGBTQ+ inclusion, childhood prejudice, or misunderstanding LGBTQ+ identities. As schools, we need to be confident in our mission, the reasons for doing DEIB work, and how to communicate this to parents in advance of curriculum changes, when complaints may arise.

The most important point to consider before we explore how to work with parents is knowing the local community. You know your community far better than I do, so rather than giving you a set of foolproof ideas, I will outline some principles of communication. You can then use these to develop a strategy that works for your school and community.

Before beginning to communicate with families, consider where your community is now. Are they ready for you to begin talking about LGBTQ+ inclusion openly? Are there pockets of the community that will struggle more than others? Are there individuals who could help you to understand their objections?

Involving parents in the process

In an ideal situation, parents will be involved at the beginning this process – for example, in making decisions such as which books to purchase, how to structure the curriculum, and at what age different concepts should be covered in RSE.

You can start this relationship by sending out surveys. (You can find an example in the Useful Resources at the end of this book.) Be clear about what you intend to find out, and do not be afraid of open questions. These can give you important information on what the community believes and feels and what potential opposition you might encounter later on.

For a more personal interaction, select key members of the community to form a group that will work with teachers on planning the development of the curriculum. A fitting and often enjoyable job for these parents is to identify inclusive texts for the school (you could even get the PTA to buy them). It is more difficult for parents to complain about the books in school if other parents chose them; plus, they are bound to find books that you have never heard of before. Although the school needs to check the selections and make the final decision, this parental contribution can help you to both stock your library and bring parents into the heart of the school.

Informing about topics and language

Although there is no requirement to inform parents in advance about inclusivity in the curriculum, I would always advise transparency, which is the best tool we have to combat misinformation. Although it might lead to additional questions from parents, being open from the beginning will ensure that any queries are dealt with before the lesson or topic begins, and any support or adjustments can be made accordingly. It is far more difficult to appease parents afterwards. Sharing book lists and topic maps is helpful for parents in many ways; tackling misinformation about the curriculum is just one of them.

Parents should have access to any resources used in the school, LGBTQ+ resources being no exception. However, that does not mean you have to start sending out every single resource in bulk or on request. This would represent an unrealistic workload in an already overloaded system. I would advise that if a parent requests to see a resource, grant that request, but ask them to come into school to see it. This also gives you the opportunity to discuss the resource and give some context on where it has come from, when it will be used, and, most importantly, why it is used.

One of the difficulties some communities have with an inclusive curriculum is the language used, which some people deem to be inappropriate. While some of the language we use is dictated by the national curriculum, not all of it is, so it can be more difficult to justify the introduction of these words to critical parents. When talking about LGBTQ+ identities, you should have a clear justification for why language is being presented at a specific time, as well as being assured in your own conviction that saying the word 'gay' is not going to turn anyone homosexual.

Making reasonable adjustments

Whether complaints are down to the cultural, religious, or personal values of families, we cannot compromise the values and ethos of the entire school because of a few individuals. However, we can make reasonable adjustments to support these families and help them to trust the school and the education we are delivering.

At the beginning of topics, sharing book lists and giving parents the opportunity to see the books can alleviate anxiety around what they may contain. Providing the context for any potentially controversial books and explaining how they are used can also help families to see that their worries may be misplaced.

Before specific lessons, particularly those around reproduction or contraception, you may feel it necessary to share vocabulary lists or even lesson plans with parents. This transparency will help most families to understand what you will be teaching.

Can I withdraw my child?

The legislation surrounding whether a child can be withdrawn from the curriculum varies from country to country, including within the UK.

In England and Scotland, pupils can be withdrawn from sex education but not from the rest of relationships education.[1] In Northern Ireland, requests are considered on a case-by-case basis.[2] In Wales, pupils cannot be withdrawn from any part of the curriculum.[3]

However, in none of these curricula are parents given the opportunity to withdraw their children from an LGBTQ+ inclusive

---

1 Department for Education, *Relationships Education, Relationships and Sex Education (RSE) and Health Education: Statutory Guidance for Governing Bodies, Proprietors, Head Teachers, Principals, Senior Leadership Teams, Teachers* (2019). Available at: https://www.gov.uk/government/publications/relationships-education-relationships-and-sex-education-rse-and-health-education; Scottish Government, *Delivery of Relationships, Sexual Health and Parenthood Education in Scottish Schools: Draft Guidance* (24 August 2023). Available at: https://www.gov.scot/publications/guidance-delivery-relationships-sexual-health-parenthood-rshp-education-scottish-schools/pages/3.
2 See https://www.education-ni.gov.uk/articles/relationship-and-sexuality-education-rse.
3 Welsh Government, *Relationships and Sexuality Education (RSE) Statutory Guidance and Code: Consultation Document* (2021), p. 7. Available at: https://www.gov.wales/sites/default/files/consultations/2021-05/consultation-document-relationships-and-sexuality-education-guidance-and-code_0.pdf.

curriculum. For example, nowhere in the UK does a parent have the right to withdraw their child from a lesson where a book with two mums is read or where pupils are learning about LGBTQ+ role models.

With regard to LGBTQ+ inclusion, where no sex education is involved, schools need to be confident in their values and not allow some parents to withdraw their children from lessons or activities that would cause no harm. Granting this would undermine the work you are doing and create a two-tier system whereby you are implying that it is acceptable to attend your school and exhibit prejudice. I recommend that you are quite firm here: when parents send pupils to your school, they are agreeing to the values of your school. If they can pick and choose, then your school values are meaningless.

While you should always stand by your school values, you do not want to antagonise your community. Holding Pride events (which I will come on to shortly) or flying Pride flags might be a step too far initially for some parents. After all, communities need to go on a journey too. However, having the baseline that your curriculum will represent the world we live in should be a minimum standard for all pupils.

In 2024, I visited a school in Darlington which has a personalised approach to the curriculum, particularly for their Traveller families. Where there are trigger points, such as during lessons about repro-duction or where there is direct teaching about LGBTQ+ inclusion, Roma and Traveller children are given the option of attending an alternate lesson. Supported by the Traveller Education and Achievement Service, the children still receive teaching on the same topic but using resources and content specifically created for Traveller families.

This might seem unusual or even appear that we are cowing to the beliefs of these families. But let me ask you this: would you prefer it if the children had a slightly modified curriculum and were in school, or were forced to take part in lessons they disagreed with and so were either absent for long periods or removed entirely? While this might not be an approach suitable for all schools, it works for this school, which is going some way to breaking the cycle of mistrust that these families have for the education system.

Writing a script

In most schools I have worked with, many teachers are worried about how they deal with parents who unexpectedly make complaints about LGBTQ+ inclusion, such as a book that is used in a topic or at story time. Teachers are often concerned about getting into an argument or saying the wrong thing, so it can be useful for you to develop a script with staff.

When I say 'script', I do not mean a word-for-word account of what you will say every time, but some guidance for teachers on what should and should not be said, and in what order.

First, look at the following complaints. Take a few minutes to think about or write down how you would respond to each of them:

+ I'm concerned that you are teaching my son to be gay.

+ I don't want you teaching any of that trans stuff in school.

+ Please take my daughter out of any lessons that have gay people in them.

+ The pupils are too young to be reading these books.

+ I don't want my children exposed to these books.

Carefully consider each of your responses. There is a good chance that they are not consistent, or you might not be entirely sure what to say. That is fine. Doing this exercise with staff can break down the concerns that people have and begin to develop a consensus on what we could include in our script.

For each answer, think about what you should start with, what point you want to make, and how you can finish if the parent is still not satisfied. Avoid getting into a debate; instead, focus on non-negotiable facts about your school.

Here is an example of a script that I created with a trust to be used across their schools:

+ You have told me ...

+ Our school values are ...

+ We are a fully inclusive school ...

+ If you would like to talk more about this ...

The script should be simple, easy to follow, and adaptable but does not allow for any argument. It is not a teacher's job to get into a debate with parents about the content of the curriculum (that is why leaders get paid the big bucks). But if every member of staff follows the same script, then parents who have complaints about these areas will soon begin to realise that the school has a unified stance.

If you are in an area with a large number of religious families, you may also want to consider working with members of places of worship, such as the local church, mosque, synagogue, or gurdwara, so you can also add to the script:

✦ The ... is supportive of this view ...

Demonstrating the unity of community and religious groups can be an effective tool in empowering your staff and ensuring that parents are getting the message that diversity and inclusion is important to everyone in your school and community.

To Pride or not to Pride

Before planning a Pride event, ask yourself and your team: 'What is Pride?' This seemingly simple question can provoke deep reflection. Pride is commonly seen as a celebration of diversity, inclusion, and individuality. However, its origins are rooted in peaceful protest and advocacy for LGBTQ+ equality. At its heart, Pride is about visibility, equality, and the fight for rights.

When considering a Pride celebration in your school, reflect on whether the event will align with this purpose or if it is simply a celebration of diversity. While both are valuable, recognising the distinction will shape your planning and help you to define your goals.

Why hold a Pride celebration?

Schools should be safe and welcoming spaces for all pupils, including those who identify as LGBTQ+. By holding a Pride event, you send a strong message of acceptance and support, helping LGBTQ+ pupils feel seen, valued, and respected. Pride events can also serve as opportunities to educate all pupils about diversity, helping to break down stereotypes and reduce bullying. As we have seen, the research shows that LGBTQ+ pupils are at a higher risk of bullying and mental-health problems, and fostering understanding is a key step towards combating these issues. Additionally, Pride provides a platform to celebrate the uniqueness of every individual. When executed thoughtfully, it can inspire a school-wide culture of acceptance and kindness. In addition, it can be a really fun day with lots of laughter and learning that brings the community together.

Concerns and challenges

While Pride focuses on LGBTQ+ inclusion, schools should also be mindful of representing other groups and identities, including those related to race, religion, and disability. A narrowly focused event could inadvertently feel exclusionary to others. Inclusivity should not be limited to a single occasion. It should be embedded throughout the curriculum and school culture. Pride celebrations should complement, not replace, ongoing efforts to create a genuinely inclusive environment.

One way of making an event such as this more inclusive is to consider not calling it Pride. We can keep the spirit of Pride and the activities that make it engaging, while also avoiding some of the community opposition that may arise from the use of the word 'Pride'. I have seen this strategy rolled out incredibly successfully in schools with event names such as Good to Be Me Day, Shine Your Colours Day, Diversity Day, and Proud to Be You Day.

To determine whether holding this type of celebration is the right decision for your school, consider why you are holding it, what you hope to achieve, how you will include all pupils and underrepresented groups, and whether you can celebrate individuality and diversity without referring to Pride. If the answers align with your school's values and goals, then this celebration could be a powerful addition to your calendar.

Making a Pride celebration successful

If you decide to move forward with an event, the key is to make it fun, inclusive, and meaningful; you do not need a drag queen to make it a success (although they can be fabulous!). Start by defining what it is you want to achieve. Whether it is celebrating individuality, promoting kindness, or raising awareness of LGBTQ+ inclusion, being clear on your goals will help you to shape your plans.

Involve the whole school community by gathering ideas from staff, pupils, and parents. You could have a parade where everyone gets to show off their creativity with costumes or banners, host a rainbow-themed bake sale, or organise a talent show that highlights the unique skills of your pupils. For younger children, enjoyable activities might include story time featuring inclusive books, creating rainbow crafts, or singing songs about friendship. Older pupils might enjoy planning an assembly, learning about LGBTQ+ history through interactive workshops, or even holding debates on diversity and inclusion.

Consider making your event about celebrating all forms of diversity to ensure that everyone feels included – for example, you could showcase cultural dances, host a food festival with dishes from different communities, or organise a talent swap where pupils teach each other skills or traditions from their backgrounds. You could also create a collaborative art project, like a mural that represents various aspects of the school community, or hold a storytelling day where pupils share family traditions or personal stories about what makes them unique. By broadening the scope of your event, you create opportunities to celebrate different cultures, abilities, and identities, while still highlighting the values of inclusion and kindness. Whatever events you choose, aim to create an occasion filled with joy and collaboration, leaving everyone feeling connected and proud to be part of your school community.

If you decide that a Pride celebration is not the right fit for your school, do not be ashamed or think that you are not being inclusive. Every school community is different, and there is no one-size-fits-all models for inclusion. You must do what is right for your pupils, teachers, school, and community.

If you do decide to hold a celebration, then I hope you have the best day – and please get in touch to let me know how it went.

Clubbing together

In a way, whether to have an LGBTQ+ club is a similar conversation to whether to hold a Pride event.

Personally, I believe that there is rarely a case to have an LGBTQ+ club in primary schools. Despite there being LGBTQ+ pupils in the school, the vast majority are likely to either not know their identity, not have come to terms with it yet, be confused, or simply not be ready to come out. This then begs the question why an LGBTQ+ club is needed. In most schools, this type of club provides a safe space, helps pupils to find allies, and offers support to young people struggling with their identity; it is unlikely that this will be of benefit to most primary children. There is also the possibility that it creates issues inadvertently, as some children may feel the need to label themselves prematurely in order to attend. There may be school-specific reasons why you need to establish an LGBTQ+ club in primary school, but it is unlikely to be useful or appropriate for most.

Pupils attending secondary schools are far more likely to come out, so many schools do run an LGBTQ+ club for the reasons mentioned above. At this age, we naturally move into groups with people with similar identities, beliefs, and values to ourselves, so an LGBTQ+ club can be a good way for these pupils to find peers, friends, and allies.

If you are considering setting up a Pride club, here are some issues to think about.

Why are you setting up a club?

This is the most important consideration. If you are establishing a club because you think you should or because a school down the road has one, then I am sorry to tell you that it is unlikely to work. If you are unclear about your motivations, it is likely to become a virtue-signalling exercise which will not align with what the pupils, the school, and the community want. Think about the following:

✤ Why does your school need an LGBTQ+ club?

✤ How do you know it is needed?

✦ What would be the potential benefits to your pupils, school, and community?

With the pupils, create a manifesto of sorts where you clearly identify the group's purpose, aims, and aspirations. This will help you to ensure that all the decisions about the club are made for a reason and everyone is moving in the same direction. This manifesto should also align with your school's vision statement on inclusion.

How, when, and where will the club run?

When we decide to set up an LGBTQ+ club, it can be tempting to become excited, plan everything, and launch it without involving the most important people in the process: the pupils. First, speak openly to LGBTQ+ young people to find out their views. The types of questions you want to ask include:

✦ Do you think an LGBTQ+ club would be beneficial for you, the school, and the community?

✦ Why do you think we do or do not need an LGBTQ+ club?

✦ If we had a club, where and when should it meet?

✦ Who would attend the club?

✦ How do we protect the identities of LGBTQ+ pupils who might want to come and are not out?

✦ What would happen at the club?

✦ Who would run the club, and how could the pupils get involved?

How do we protect the identities of members of the club?

The irony of having an open LGBTQ+ club is that sometimes the people you would like to attend will not because they are not out. I certainly would not have gone to an LGBTQ+ club if there was one in my school because I would have been terrified of the bullying I was already receiving getting worse. More importantly, it would have meant a step towards accepting my identity for which I just wasn't ready. To get around these problems, it is essential that the club is not an LGBTQ+ exclusive club but is also open to allies. In this way, if someone attends who is not yet out, they will be in an environment where there are other perceived non-LGBTQ+ people, so there is less likely to be an assumption that everyone who attends is LGBTQ+.

You will also need to consider when and where the club will be located. It needs to be somewhere away from the main flow of the school; not to hide it away but to give young people the anonymity of going if they are nervous. There is no right or wrong about when to hold it but consider when during the day would allow people to attend without drawing attention to themselves.

Hiding the club away might seem to go against being proud of who we are, but if only people who are proudly open attend, then we have to question the true purpose of the club.

What happens in an LGBTQ+ club?

The answer to this question partially lies in another question: what is the purpose of the club? At a very basic level, the club can be a safe space for people to get to know each other, to chat, and to find people like them – or, indeed, different from them.

An LGBTQ+ club is a brilliant place to raise awareness of events such as LGBTQ+ History Month and Pride Month, hold discussions, create displays, and act as a driving force behind inclusion in the school. When planning what happens in an LGBTQ+ club, listen to all your pupils, not just the ones who attend. Sometimes the people we want to attend are the ones who are not yet willing to come, so the activities need to be designed to support and encourage them.

Should it just be an LGBTQ+ club?

Sometimes, there is a perception that schools give more support to LGBTQ+ pupils than other minorities, such as those of different faiths, global majority backgrounds, or with disabilities or neurodivergence. You need to consider whether these pupils also have a safe space to go, and if not, why not?

I have worked with many schools which have decided that, rather than setting up an LGBTQ+ or Pride club, to create a club or safe space that is welcoming to everyone and supports and celebrates all diversity. I saw a perfect example of this at a school in Swansea, South Wales, where the Prism Club created artworks about people who inspired them. It featured music, paintings, sculpture, films, and many other mediums about inspiring people of different cultures, religions, genders, sexualities, and with various disabilities. It was incredibly moving to see so many parents coming into school to see the work on diversity.

Although your priority in reading this book might be LGBTQ+ pupils, I would also urge you to think wider than that. You could create something really special here!

Awards season

When I was teaching in the early 2010s (showing my age here), there seemed to be an unofficial competition between schools about how many award badges would appear at the bottom of the letterhead and on the school website. If you saw a school with a badge you did not have, that was it; it went into next year's school improvement plan. In the early days of school awards, they were incredibly useful and provided a framework for improvement. Later on, they became a tick-box exercise about proving what you were already doing rather than helping the school to improve.

More recently, I have seen a reduction in the number of awards that schools are going for, but also a move back towards using awards as a tool for improvement. Whether this is due to changes in attitudes, time constraints, falling school budgets, or a combination of them all, is unclear. If you do decide to try for an award for inclusion, I would urge you to go for one that you feel will make the biggest difference to your school – not to get a badge for your website but as a tool for school improvement.

Chapter 9
Not All Heroes Wear Capes

. . . .

It was 3 January 2023, and it was my first day of not being a teacher for almost 20 years. I had begun the first day of my six-month sabbatical, and I was sitting at my laptop asking myself what on earth I had done. I don't really think that imposter syndrome begins to describe what I felt that day. What if I didn't get any work? How would I pay the mortgage? Was I even qualified for this work?

The reality is that I had spent the last six months preparing for this. I had read every LGBTQ+ inclusion book I could get my hands on, arranged meetings with more LGBTQ+ activists and educators than I even knew existed, read dozens of research papers on safeguarding and effective RSE, and built a website and training package of which I was really proud. I can't say that it had ever crossed my mind that this is where my teaching career would lead. However, I knew why I was doing this. I kept thinking back to what I had been through in school and that I felt a responsibility to those young people who needed support.

Then, without warning, came my first invitation into a school. A friend from university contacted me about running some workshops for pupils and delivering staff training. Honestly, the day couldn't have gone any better. The pupils were so receptive – we unpicked why using gay as an insult had to stop. The staff were equally enthusiastic and left with a clear plan of what needed to change in their school. I still work with the school, but it was incredible to hear that six months after my visit they had a 90% reduction in homophobic language. I'm really proud of them for the work they put in, but you know what, I'm going to give myself a rare pat on the back here and say, 'Well done Ian – you did a cracking job.'

A remarkable thing happened then. Word spread, and before long I was working in schools across the country delivering training and workshops. Each time I visited a school, I developed and refined the work, and I began to make strong partnerships and relationships all over the UK. It was all going so well.

But as my social-media following grew, so did the attention – and not the good kind. I started to see a different side of social media that I had only heard about before. A tweet about something as innocuous as wearing a poppy could result in accusations, outright lies, and truly disgusting comments about my identity and my intentions. It really got to me in the early days. But as time went on, I have accepted that these vile comments say more about the trolls than they do about me. They never take the time to find out what I actually do. When they do ask, they don't want to know the answer; they just want to spread negativity, hostility, and conspiracy theories. And so, I no longer engage (or I try not to) and focus instead on spreading positivity.

It would be easy for me to give up this work because of anonymous social-media trolls and bigoted people who can't see out of their echo chambers, but I will not stop until our society is truly equal. In April 2024, I set up More Than Flags and Rainbows, a not-for-profit that is our vehicle for all the change that I have set out in this book. We work with organisations across the UK and are already beginning to see the dial move in places where we have collaborated. In a way, it's my dream that More Than Flags and Rainbows isn't needed in the future. Until then, I'll keep championing the people who need our help and fighting against the prejudice that does not belong in modern Britain.

It's been a bit of a wild ride, and I cannot thank you enough for reading on. This brings us to the end of my story and on to yours.

· ·

As we reach the final chapter of this book, it is time to reflect on what it truly means to be a leader in diversity and inclusion. You have read through the strategies, the tips, and the practical advice on how to promote inclusivity in your school. However, leading change is difficult. It is not always filled with motivational quotes and breakthrough moments. It involves long days, challenging conversations, and moments of doubt that may leave you questioning whether it is all worth it. And the truth is, it *is* worth it, but only if you can maintain your own well-being along the way.

Being a leader is similar to being a superhero but without the cape. You are expected to advocate for fairness, challenge the status quo, and ensure that every pupil and staff member feels seen, supported, and valued. But, just like any leader, you cannot do it alone, and you certainly cannot do it if you are running on empty. This chapter is dedicated to you – those leading the charge for change in your school. It is about recognising the emotional, mental, and physical toll that this work can take on you and offering some much-needed advice on how to keep going without burning out or losing sight of your well-being.

Whether you are navigating resistance, facing online criticism, or trying to balance the demands of the job with your own mental health, this chapter will provide guidance on how to stay grounded. You do not have to do everything. You do not need to have all the answers. And, most importantly, you do not have to sacrifice yourself for the cause. We will consider whether LGBTQ+ teachers and staff should come out; what to do if you, the school, or members of staff face abuse or criticism; the importance of self-care; and what should be in your inclusion toolkit.

First, let us explore how to lead with integrity, drive change with purpose, and do it all while maintaining our well-being – because effective leaders prioritise their own health while working to create positive change.

Caring for yourself

Leading DEIB change in a school is both rewarding and exhausting. It requires not just a deep commitment to justice and fairness but also an incredible amount of emotional and mental energy. As a DEIB leader, you will often be at the forefront of conversations about inequality, discrimination, and societal issues that affect your pupils and colleagues. While this work is essential, it also comes with its own set of challenges that can take a toll on your well-being.

The emotional weight of the work is the primary reason why DEIB leaders need to prioritise self-care. Every day, you are navigating difficult topics like racism, sexism, homophobia, and ableism. You are listening to the stories of pupils and staff who have experienced hurt and exclusion. While this is important work, it is also draining. The constant need to process these emotions, provide support, and guide others along their own journeys of understanding can lead to compassion fatigue. The risk here is that, over time, the emotional burden of constantly addressing the needs of others can leave you feeling overwhelmed and disconnected from your own needs.

Another significant challenge is the resistance you may face. Not everyone will be open to the changes you are advocating, and some may actively push back against your efforts. This resistance can come in many forms, from subtle microaggressions to open hostility. It is not only frustrating, but it can also be disheartening. When your work is met with opposition, it can feel like you are con-stantly fighting an uphill battle. This can lead to burnout, and the drive to create change can come to feel like a heavy burden rather than a motivating force.

Additionally, the sheer volume of work that comes with being a DEIB leader can be overwhelming. You are often balancing multi-ple responsibilities, from planning and delivering training to meeting with staff, pupils, and parents, to implementing policies and monitoring progress. The burden of these tasks, combined with the emotional labour, can lead to a constant feeling of being 'on', with little opportunity for rest. When you are always working to improve the school environment for others, it can be difficult to carve out time for yourself. The pressure to always be available and constantly work for the greater good can leave you with little room to prioritise your own health.

Finally, there is the personal cost of this work. As a leader, you may be publicly associated with the changes you are championing. This can bring both praise and criticism, and when the criticism is harsh or personal, it can take a toll on your self-esteem and mental health. The emotional impact of handling a public backlash, especially when it is based on misunderstandings or personal attacks, can feel isolating. If you are constantly defending your work or your values, it is easy to lose sight of your own well-being.

I do not want to put you off, but I do not hear enough talk about how working on inclusion impacts on well-being. To be effective in your role as a leader, you must ensure that you are in a position where you can continue to support others without depleting yourself. Prioritising self-care helps you to maintain the emotional resilience needed to navigate the challenges of leadership. It allows you to recharge and refocus, ensuring that you can stay motivated and effective in the long term. This work is important, but so is your health. The more you take care of yourself, the better equipped you will be to lead, inspire, and create lasting change.

Self-care looks different for every leader, but it involves finding ways to recharge physically, emotionally, and mentally. One key aspect is building a supportive team around you. You do not have to shoulder everything alone. Whether it is delegating tasks, seeking mentorship, or building a network of allies within the school, having others to share the load with can make a significant difference. This reduces the pressure on you and ensures that you have people to turn to when challenges arise.

Another essential practice is giving yourself space. Set boundaries and allow yourself to take breaks, even when the work feels neverending. This could mean taking short walks, doing breathing exercises, or stepping away from difficult conversations to clear your mind. It also includes scheduling regular time off to fully disconnect from work. This space helps you to recharge, preventing the feeling of being overwhelmed.

Celebrating small victories is a crucial part of self-care. The journey can often feel slow, but acknowledging each step forward – from positive feedback after a training session to the smallest shift in school culture – can fuel your motivation. Take time to reflect on what you have achieved, even when progress seems incremental.

Nurturing your physical health is vital too. Regular exercise, a balanced diet, and sufficient sleep are fundamental to maintaining the energy needed for the work you do. It might sound like a cliché, but physical health has a direct impact on mental resilience, so prioritising your health should be non-negotiable.

Lastly, seeking professional support when needed is essential. This work can bring up heavy emotions, and talking to a therapist or coach can provide you with the tools to process these feelings and stay balanced.

Self-care is not a luxury but a necessity. By building a strong support system, setting boundaries, prioritising your physical health, celebrating progress, and taking time for reflection, you can ensure that you lead with energy, resilience, and purpose.

Out of the closet and into the fire

If you are LGBTQ+ and work in a school, it has no doubt crossed your mind how public you choose to be about your identity. If you are not LGBTQ+, it may not have occurred to you, but you have probably come out without realising it. If you have mentioned your girlfriend/boyfriend or wife/husband, even in passing, or have a picture of your family on your desk, then you have actually come out as straight. The narrative that straight people do not come out is a myth.

The reality of the world we live in means that for a teacher being public about an LGBTQ+ identity is more complicated than for those who are not LGBTQ+. When working with LGBTQ+ staff – or, indeed, if this applies to you – we need to consider whether the school is a place to be public and, if so, how it should be done.

The first point to acknowledge is that sexuality is a protected characteristic, and therefore it is illegal to discriminate against someone because of it. This means that opportunities cannot be restricted, and staff should not suffer discrimination because of their sexual orientation or gender identity.

Aside from the obvious concern about acceptance, some LGBTQ+ teachers are worried that being open about their sexuality will contradict the guidance or policies of their school. For example, the guidance in England states that teachers should demonstrate 'political impartiality'.[1] This guidance has faced criticism from many

---

1   Department for Education and N. Zahawi, Political Impartiality in Schools (17 February 2022). Available at: https://www.gov.uk/government/publications/political-impartiality-in-schools.

sectors as it is fraught with problems. Who deems what is impartial? Does this mean that teachers must hide their opinions about every little thing? School vision statements are not impartial documents, as they drive an agenda that seeks to improve the school, the community, and the life of all stakeholders, so do they have to be scrapped?

While it is a fair point that we need to be careful that schools are not pushing harmful agendas, one of the reasons that this guidance has been decried is that it harks back to the time of Section 28, when the 'promotion' of homosexuality was banned in schools. On social media, I have read posts by newly qualified teachers concerned that if they come out to their pupils, they are not being impartial and therefore not adhering to the guidance.

But impartiality suggests that sexuality is a choice rather than part of someone's identity. Being a member of the Labour Party and a socialist and believing in removing Church from state are aspects of my personal belief system and can be changed by conscious choice. They are not protected, therefore, and I should not be pushing these views on to the children in my classroom. However, my sexuality is part of who I am, and if I choose to share this information, I should not be required to hide it. To do so would propel us back to a time where many teachers and pupils (including myself) felt the need to repress who they were, causing a multitude of societal and mental-health issues. We would not expect someone to hide their sex, race, disability, or religion, so asking people to hide their sexuality is tantamount to oppression and directly contravenes the Equality Act 2010.

Of course, some people have concerns about the word 'sexuality' being used in schools. Obviously, we do not want to be talking about sex with pupils before they are developmentally ready to understand it, but there is no need to if a teacher chooses to come out. I have come out to every class I have taught for the last 10 years, but I have not once talked about sex while doing so. I always start the school year by showing my class a picture of my family: my partner and adopted son. I do not make a big issue out of it; I just share that this is my family. This subtle way of coming out means that I am not discussing sex in any way, but sharing the photograph means that I can be a more authentic version of myself and enables the classroom and school to be more inclusive. If anyone is concerned about sharing that they are in a same-sex relationship, consider whether other school staff have mentioned that they are in a heterosexual relationship by revealing that they are married? If yes, then a gay or bisexual teacher has every right to share information about their family too.

A common trope used by opponents of LGBTQ+ visibility in primary schools is that there is an agenda of 'queering' the education system. It is true that we do not have a full understanding of what the biological mechanisms are that result in different sexualities, but what is clear is that being LGBTQ+ is not a choice. Having LGBTQIA+ role models in schools may result in more pupils coming out, but this is not because they are being converted (which is not possible anyway). Rather, these pupils feel that the school ethos allows them to be honest about who they are, which is a wonderful thing. There is no conspiracy of queering education but, as educators (and as humane people), we want our pupils to grow up being comfortable and confident with who they are.

With all of this comes the caveat that any teacher thinking about coming out should consider the community of their school. An individual school or community may be affected by latent homophobia, biphobia, or transphobia, potentially stemming from religious or societal reasons, so the individual should first become familiar with the views of the community. Teachers should not put themselves at risk. If your school is in an area where this might be an issue, staff should talk to their head teacher to discuss how they can come out in a carefully constructed and graduated way. Homophobia, biphobia, and transphobia are never acceptable, but we need to acknowledge that some people need to be educated first, and that approaching this matter in the wrong way could cause more animosity in the school community. In my first school, it took me several years to come out; I allowed the community to get to know me first. Although that is not the way it should be, unfortunately, that is the way our society works in some places.

Your school's equalities policy should cover staff as well as pupils. Look at this policy carefully and identify how it supports members of staff to be their authentic selves. A teacher sharing that they are in a same-sex relationship should not be an issue. It can even be a powerful tool to enable staff to become role models to LGBTQ+ pupils and help others broaden their horizons. Schools should never stop a member of staff or pupil from being themselves, but carefully considering how best to approach coming out can avoid problems that may arise from other stakeholders mistaking this honesty for an agenda or being in conflict with their personal beliefs.

Swimming against the current

The level of support for inclusion initiatives will vary significantly across different schools and can shape your ability to enact meaningful change. Some schools may already have a strong commitment to inclusivity, with senior leaders and staff fully on board, while others may be less receptive to these efforts. Within this spectrum, you may find varying degrees of resistance, indifference, or genuine interest, so understanding where your school sits will help you to navigate the challenges of promoting diversity and inclusion. Your approach and strategy will need to be adaptable, taking into account the support or opposition you face from leadership, staff, and the wider school community.

I am going to be very honest with you here. If you are not in a senior leadership role and find that the SLT does not support the changes you are trying to implement, the impact you will have is going to be limited. Without the backing of senior leaders, it can be difficult to create lasting change, as only they have the authority to influence policies, resources, and priorities within the school. In this situation, it is crucial to find ways to engage with the SLT in a constructive manner. Start by building a strong case for why diversity and inclusion is essential for the school's overall development. Provide data, research, and examples of how inclusive practices benefit both pupils and staff.

One of the most effective ways of doing this is through pupil voice. If pupils are telling the SLT that they do not feel safe, or are facing bullying, or are unhappy, it should be hard for leaders not to pay attention. (See Chapter 3 for how to collect this information.)

Try to align your goals with the broader goals of the school, such as improving pupil well-being, academic achievement, and the school's reputation. By demonstrating how these initiatives can support the school's mission, you make it harder for the SLT to dismiss the importance of these efforts. Additionally, consider framing this work as a necessary aspect of modern education, helping the school to stay relevant and competitive. The key is to show that inclusive practices are not an add-on but a fundamental part of the school's success.

Building relationships with key members of SLT, even those who may not be supportive initially, can help you to gain their trust and slowly shift their mindset. Invest time in understanding their priorities and concerns and frame your DEIB initiatives in a way that addresses them. Approach members of the SLT with respect, recognising that change is a gradual process. By cultivating strong professional relationships, you may eventually be able to alter their thinking and gain the support needed to make real change.

Do not underestimate the power of small wins. Even if the steps you take are minor initially, celebrate them and use them to demonstrate the effectiveness of DEIB work. These small victories can be used as evidence when approaching the SLT to show that these initiatives have a tangible and positive impact. Over time, these incremental changes can create momentum, building a case for more significant changes.

If the lack of support persists, it might be worth exploring other avenues, such as connecting with staff, pupils, or parents to activate a bottom-up movement for change. Creating a groundswell of support from these groups can place pressure on the SLT to reconsider their stance and may persuade the leadership to take notice and reconsider their position.

It can be a particularly challenging situation if a new head teacher is appointed who is not on board with your DEIB efforts. A head teacher has the power to shape the direction of the school, so could hinder (or significantly advance) diversity and inclusion initiatives. In this case, approach the situation with openness and diplomacy. Take the time to understand their perspective. They may have different priorities or may not yet fully understand the importance of inclusive practices. It is helpful to remain patient, as a new leader may need time to get to know the existing culture and dynamics. Give them a chance to acclimatise to the school before pushing too hard for change. They may also need time to gain the trust of the staff and to understand the specific needs of the school community.

However, if it becomes clear that diversity and inclusion is not a priority for either the school or the head teacher, you may need to assess whether it is possible to work within these constraints. Take a step back and assess whether staying in that environment is the right decision for you. I truly empathise with the difficult position this may put you in; you have a deep passion for making a difference and leaving could feel like abandoning a valuable cause. However, your well-being must come first. If you are in a school where your values are not supported or where your efforts to create a more inclusive and equitable space are being ignored or undermined, it can quickly take a toll on your mental and emotional health.

No matter how much you want to make a change, you cannot do this alone. If the situation is becoming too toxic or draining, staying in a school that does not align with your principles may not be sustainable. You deserve to work in an environment where your contributions are valued and where you can make a meaningful impact without sacrificing your own well-being. Sometimes, moving on to a different role or school can be the most courageous and responsible decision, not just for your career but for your own peace of mind and long-term happiness.

Stronger together

At those times when you need support, whether that is advice on a difficult situation, someone to advocate on your behalf, or simply reassurance that you are not alone in your experiences, unions can play a vital role. Having the backing of a union can be the difference between feeling isolated and having the confidence to challenge unfair practices.

Unions are often the first port of call when you are facing workplace issues, as they operate helplines where you can speak to experienced professionals about anything from contract disputes to safeguarding concerns. These helplines can provide practical advice, helping you to navigate difficult conversations with leadership or advising you on your legal rights. Whether it is an issue of discrimination, excessive workload, or a safeguarding dilemma, knowing you have expert guidance at the other end of a phone can be invaluable.

Many unions have dedicated LGBTQ+ networks, providing a space for educators to connect, share experiences, and campaign for better inclusion in the profession. These groups can offer practical resources, guidance on dealing with homophobia, biphobia, or transphobia in the workplace, and opportunities to be part of wider movements advocating for systemic change. They also offer an essential sense of community, ensuring that you do not feel like you are fighting these battles alone. I am part of several WhatsApp groups including National Education Union and NAHT groups, and they have been an invaluable source of solidarity, advice, and social support.

Beyond workplace advocacy, unions also organise social events and conferences, giving you the chance to meet like-minded colleagues and build support networks outside your immediate school environment. These events can be especially important if you are in a setting where you feel isolated in your views or where inclusion is not a priority. Being around others who understand the challenges you face can be both reassuring and motivating, reminding you that change is possible.

Unions also provide online resources, from guidance documents and model policies to webinars on key topics. If you need to know how to challenge a discriminatory policy, respond to homophobic bullying, or simply understand your rights as an educator, these materials can save you hours of searching for reliable information. They also offer training opportunities, helping you to develop the skills to advocate effectively for yourself and others.

The reality is that, no matter how dedicated you are, you cannot take on systemic issues alone. Having the backing of a union means that you have access to legal support, collective action, and a wider network of people fighting for the same causes. If your school is resistant to change, your union can give you the tools and confidence to keep pushing forward – or the support you need if you decide it is time to move on. No one should have to fight for inclusion alone, and with the right backing, you never have to.

The teacher in heels

Right, we are almost at the end of the book and so it is time to tell you about the heels and how wearing them led me to start this work. Many people know me as the teacher in heels after a photo went viral in 2022. My class were designing clothes for a fashion show and one of my pupils dared me to wear heels for the catwalk. We had a lot of conversations about gender stereotypes and the history of clothing, and so I did it.

After a lot (and I mean *a lot*) of practice at home strutting down my hallway to RuPaul tracks, I was ready. We did the fashion show, and I powered down that catwalk, channelling the swagger of the model Kate Moss and the attitude of a seasoned drag queen. I looked fierce. The kids loved it. The parents loved it. We took a photo and shared it with the world to show a bit of joy after the lockdowns that had preceded the event.

I did not expect what happened next. Within hours, the photo had thousands of likes and supportive comments on Twitter. From affirmations of challenging stereotypes to questions about how well I walked, it was wonderful. Until it was not. Very quickly, the tone changed. I was attacked through replies and direct messages with insults, accusations (that I will not go into here), and even threats.

The vile remarks escalated to a point where the legal team at the local authority had to give me and my head teacher advice on how to proceed. We deleted the post and reported many of the comments. Twitter took swift action and suspended several accounts, the legal team prepared for any backlash against the school, and my head teacher was incredibly supportive.

But there was one thing missing: not once did my employer check in on me. Not a phone call. Not an email. The comments made to me were incredibly triggering, but my well-being was not a priority for the local authority. Despite support from my school, the lack of concern from my employer left me feeling far from safe, seen, and supported.

There is a lot to unpack and learn here.

First, it shows that we live in a world where a small proportion of the population have such narrow views that they believe putting on a pair of heels makes you a risk to children. It can be easy to capitulate to these people, but their extreme views are in no way representative of the majority. It is important when you start DEIB work that you do not let these extremist views stop you from helping every pupil to feel safe, seen, and supported.

Second, if you do get backlash because of your work, take a step back and analyse why it happened and who the negative reaction is coming from. There have definitely been situations where schools have moved too quickly for their community and faced criticism and even protests about their diversity work. In these cases, I would argue that it was the school's fault for not working closely enough with the community and going on the journey together. But if the reaction is from people who are in no way relevant to your school or community, as in my example, as tough as it can be, we have to remember that they are not from the area where we are working, and in the grand scheme of things, these people are not as important as our pupils and families.

Finally, we need to remember the people who are at the centre of these incidents. For many teachers from minority or underrepresented groups, episodes like this are not upsetting because of what is happening at the time but often because it triggers past traumas of bullying. This was certainly the case for me. The abuse I received meant that, for the first time in 10 years, I needed to attend therapy. We must look after our staff, not just for what they are going through now but also for what they have been through in the past.

I do not regret what I did. In fact, the abuse I received was part of the impetus I needed to encourage me to leave teaching and start More Than Flags and Rainbows (plus, I looked fabulous!). We live in a world where societal equality has not yet been reached, and I am so pleased that you have joined me on this journey so that we can create a world where every person is accepted for who they are, not what a small proportion of the population want them to be.

Beyond the rainbow

Throughout this book, you have considered how your school community can learn and grow. Using the three pillars of safe, seen, and supported, we can create an inclusive school environment where every pupil can thrive.

✚ **Safe.** Developing your understanding of LGBTQ+ vocabulary and concepts is the first step towards building a school culture where all pupils feel secure and accepted. By addressing bullying head-on and equipping yourself with the language and tools to intervene effectively, you can create a foundation of safety that enables LGBTQ+ pupils to be themselves without fear.

✚ **Seen.** Representation matters, and it is crucial that all pupils see themselves reflected positively in their learning environment. Take some time to choose appropriate and meaningful role models along with texts and images that reflect a broad spectrum of identities. By carefully selecting resources that showcase diversity, you send a powerful message that everyone has a place in the school community.

✚ **Supported.** Supporting pupils through their own journeys – such as coming out – requires sensitivity and collaboration with families. It is important that you continually reflect on how you are working with parents, understanding their concerns, and respecting each family's context. Do not worry what a school down the road is doing; think about whether a Pride event or LGBTQ+ club is right for your school. And if you do go ahead with one, carefully consider how you are working with the people who these activities will affect the most.

Inclusivity is not a one-time effort or something to tick off a list. True inclusivity lives and breathes in every decision, policy, and interaction you share with pupils. My hope is that this book has helped you to cultivate an enduring commitment to inclusivity, one that will continue to evolve with you and with each new group of pupils who walk through your doors. This commitment will carry on as you revisit, re-evaluate, and refine your approach over time. This is what makes your role so powerful, transformative, and invaluable – because you are constantly adapting to ensure that every child feels that they belong.

Whether you are a teacher, head teacher, pastoral lead, or any other part of the school community, you are uniquely placed to shape the experiences of young people, both academically and personally. Your influence reaches beyond the curriculum to affect how pupils see themselves and their peers. Through your commitment to fostering a safe and inclusive environment, you are helping every pupil, especially LGBTQ+ young people, to feel validated and valued. While you may not see the effects of each small action, every moment of acceptance and support leaves a lasting impact. Please, never underestimate the difference you are making.

This book was not always easy to write. Revisiting painful experiences brought up emotions I have often tried to leave behind, but I believe that we need to remove the stigma around sharing difficult moments. Talking about these experiences openly can help to create a path forward for others who may feel alone or unsupported. I hope my story has resonated with you and reinforced the importance of the work you are doing.

So, now is the time to take action. Find out where your school is, how life is for your pupils, and what you need to do to change things for the better for them. If you would like any support along the way, I would be glad to help however I can. But I would also love to hear about your success stories, no matter how small or big they feel. I also want to be a resource for those challenging moments when progress feels difficult or unclear. Inclusivity is a journey, and it is one we are all walking together. Please do not hesitate to reach out.

This book represents the culmination of so much of my work until now, yet it also feels like just the beginning. More Than Flags and Rainbows continues to grow as a project and as a community, and together we are building a world where no child feels isolated or unseen. This work is ongoing, and I am excited to continue it with you, learning from each other and reaching more pupils with every step.

Useful Resources

What the LGBTQIA+? answers

Here are the answers to the quiz, with a bit more information on each of them.

1. d. Asexual

Someone who does not experience sexual attraction to others, or who has a low or absent interest in sexual activity. Asexuality is distinct from celibacy or abstinence, which are choices, whereas asexuality in an identity. People who identify as asexual may still experience romantic attraction and they may go through periods of varying sexual levels of attraction.

2. c. Bisexual

This describes a person who is attracted to more than one sex or gender. Bisexual individuals may experience sexual or romantic attraction to both their own sex or gender and other sexes or genders. There is a lot of stigma surrounding bisexuality, particularly if a person has never been in a relationship with people of more than one sex or gender. Just because someone has not been in a relationship with a woman, does not mean that they are not attracted to them.

3. a. Gay

Okay, this was a tricky one, but the clue was the first part of the sentence. Gay is generally used to describe men who are attracted to men, but some women who are attracted to women also use it either interchangeably or in place of lesbian. This can be for flexibility, but some women feel that lesbian holds a stereotypical image and so prefer to use gay.

4. d. Transgender

This is someone whose gender does not align with the sex they were assigned at birth. There is a misconception that all transgender people undergo gender reassignment surgery, but many do not. The term transsexual is now a politically incorrect term because while all transgender people align their life with their gender, not all transgender people receive medical interventions.

5. a. Sapphic and d. Lesbian

I bet I caught most of you out there! If you got both of them, you get a bonus point. Both sapphic and lesbian mean women who are attracted to women but with a slight nuanced difference. Generally, lesbian refers to women who are only attracted to women, while sapphic can also include women who are bisexual or pansexual.

Interesting history note: sapphic descends from the poet Sappho who lived on the island of Lesbos (isn't this amazing?). Although it is an Ancient Greek word, it was not popularised in this context until much later, although it is not exactly clear when. However, its use is now becoming very common, particularly among young people and in literary circles.

6. a. Cisgender

I am male and a man; as these match, I am cisgender. In simple terms, being cisgender is the opposite of transgender, so your gender matches your sex. It is likely that most people reading this book will be cisgender but have never used the word. For most people, they do not have any need to use this term, and its use has only arisen to distinguish areas such as transgender healthcare.

7. a. Queer

Queer is a complex term but one that is becoming increasingly important to the LGBT+ community. Meaning different things to different people, queer can be a way of describing someone's sexuality, gender, or both. It can be used either interchangeably with terms such as lesbian, bisexual, or gay, or can (although I have issues with this) be used to describe the whole LGBT+ community. Some people also use it as a broad term as they do not feel that they fit into the existing labels. The reclaiming of the word queer offers a fascinating way of viewing how LGBTQ+ rights have progressed.

8. d. Intersex

Our sex is generally defined by three aspects: hormones, chromosomes, and genitals and reproductive organs. For someone who is intersex, one of these aspects does not align with what we would expect from their sex. Although rare, their genitals may not appear to be male or female. For example, it is likely that an intersex female will have very high levels of testosterone. This has implications for sport, so during the Paris 2024 Olympics there was significant controversy surrounding Algeria's Imane Khelif who received criticism for being able to compete in the women's boxing events, despite having XY chromosomes. This demonstrates why 'sex' is not as simple as some people (particularly on social media) would have you believe. Despite this, people still have a legal sex, and male or female will be defined on your birth certificate.

As a side note, there is a debate among some about whether our sex is *observed* or *assigned* at birth. Essentially, the disagreement here is whether sex can solely be determined by the genitalia or whether it is more complex than that. I am not here to state which is correct, as not even the experts can agree, but in this book I will be using sex as assigned at birth, as this is in keeping with the language used by the UK's National Health Service.

9. c. Pansexual

Someone who identifies as pansexual is attracted to individual people, regardless of their sex, gender, or sexual orientation. There is quite a lot of overlap with bisexuality, with the difference being that someone who is bisexual may not be attracted to all gender identities. This is a great example of how, as humans, we like to label everything but not everyone fits neatly into the boxes.

10. a. Differences in sex development

In recent years, intersex conditions have been described by some as disorders of sex development or differences in sex development (DSD). However, this remains a controversial term, and outside of clinical settings, intersex remains the most widely used term.

11. a. Non-binary

Non-binary individuals may identify as having a gender that is a blend of both, neither, or a different gender altogether. Non-binary people may use a variety of pronouns, including they/them, he/him, she/her, or others, and although there can be an overlap with transgender identities, they may or may not choose to undergo medical or social transitions. There are examples of non-binary identities throughout history; it is the vocabulary that has changed, not the identity. A few decades ago, we might have described non-binary people as androgynous, but this has evolved as some non-binary people may present as men or women or be inter-changeable with their appearance. It could be argued that we should all be non-binary because wouldn't it be great for everyone to just be themselves and not be restricted by their sex. Although non-binary people do not identify as men or women, they still have a legal sex which will be male or female.

Example surveys

Example staff survey

✦ How confident are you in your understanding of common LGBTQ+ terms (e.g. bisexual, transgender, non-binary, asexual)?

Scale: very confident, somewhat confident, neutral, not very confident, not confident at all

✦ How comfortable are you discussing LGBTQ+ topics with pupils, with colleagues, and with parents?

Scale: very comfortable, somewhat comfortable, neutral, not very comfortable, not comfortable at all

✦ Have you received any prior training on LGBTQ+ inclusion in education?

Yes/no

✦ If yes, was the training useful? Why or why not?

✦ What, if anything, do you feel holds you back from confidently supporting LGBTQ+ inclusion in school? *(open-ended)*

✦ How confident do you feel handling scenarios such as: addressing a pupil being bullied for their gender identity or sexual orientation, supporting a pupil who has come out to you, and correcting colleagues or pupils on inappropriate language (e.g. 'That's so gay')?

Scale: very confident, somewhat confident, neutral, not very confident, not confident at all

✦ Are there any LGBTQ+ topics or terms you feel you do not fully understand but would like to learn more about? *(open-ended)*

✦ Do you feel that our school environment currently supports LGBTQ+ pupils effectively? Why or why not? *(open-ended)*

✦ Do you believe that LGBTQ+ inclusion is an important part of creating a positive school culture?

Scale: strongly agree, agree, neutral, disagree, strongly disagree

✦ Why do you feel this way? *(open-ended)*

- ✚ What format do you think would work best for LGBTQ+ inclusion training? Check all that apply.
  - ❯ Whole-school training.
  - ❯ Small-group discussions.
  - ❯ Online modules.
  - ❯ Practical workshops.
- ✚ Is there anything else you would like to share about your confidence, concerns, or thoughts on LGBTQ+ inclusion in our school? *(open-ended)*

Example secondary school pupil survey

This survey is anonymous and is designed to help us understand how inclusive and supportive our school is for everyone. Please answer honestly – your feedback is very important.

+ How confident are you that you understand what LGBTQ+ means?

  Scale: very confident, somewhat confident, neutral, not very confident, not confident at all

+ Do you feel comfortable talking about LGBTQ+ topics at school, with your teachers, and with your classmates?

  Scale: very comfortable, somewhat comfortable, neutral, not very comfortable, not comfortable at all

+ Do you feel like pupils at this school are respectful towards LGBTQ+ people? Why or why not? *(open-ended)*

+ Have you ever learned about LGBTQ+ topics in lessons at school?

  Yes/no

+ If yes, what topics did you learn about? *(open-ended)*

+ Do you hear phrases like 'That's so gay' or similar language being used in school? If so, where and how often?

  Scale: every day, a few times a week, occasionally, rarely, never

+ How confident would you feel reporting bullying or disrespectful behaviour related to someone's sexual orientation or gender identity?

  Scale: very confident, somewhat confident, neutral, not very confident, not confident at all

+ Do you feel there is a trusted adult at school you could talk to about LGBTQ+ topics or concerns?

  Yes/no

+ If yes, who would that be? *(open-ended)*

+ How inclusive do you think our school is for LGBTQ+ pupils?

  Scale: very inclusive, somewhat inclusive, neutral, not very inclusive, not inclusive at all

✚ Why do you feel this way? *(open-ended)*

✚ What changes, if any, do you think the school could make to become more welcoming for LGBTQ+ pupils? *(open-ended)*

✚ Is there anything else you would like to share about your experiences or thoughts regarding LGBTQ+ inclusion in our school? *(open-ended)*

Example primary school pupil survey

This survey is suitable for age 7 and up. For younger pupils, you may wish to delete certain questions or remove the open-ended sections. It may be beneficial to complete this in small groups, although you would need to ensure that certain pupils are not leading others.

This survey will help us to understand how our school can be a welcoming and happy place for everyone. Your answers are anonymous, so please be honest.

✚ Do you think it is important that all kinds of families feel welcome at school?

Yes/no/not sure

✚ Have you seen books, pictures, or activities in school that show different types of families (e.g. families with two mums, two dads, grandparents, foster families)?

Yes/no/not sure

✚ How do you feel when you hear people talking about families that are different from your own?

Options: happy, sad, interested, curious, confused, I don't mind, I don't know, other

✚ Why did you choose that answer? *(open-ended)*

✚ Have you ever heard someone say unkind things about someone else's family?

Yes/no/not sure

✚ If yes, what happened? *(open-ended)*

✚ Have you ever been bullied at school?

Yes/no/not sure

✚ If yes, what happened, and how did it make you feel? *(open-ended)*

✚ Have you ever heard someone use the word 'gay' to say something mean or unkind?

Yes/no/not sure

✚ If yes, how did it make you feel, and what did you do? *(open-ended)*

✤ If someone was being unkind to you or another pupil, do you feel you could tell a teacher or another trusted adult?

Yes/no/not sure

✤ Do you think our school does a good job of making everyone feel included, no matter what their family is like or who they are?

Scale: very good, quite good, neutral, not very good, not good at all

✤ Why do you think that? *(open-ended)*

✤ Have you ever learned about different types of families in lessons, books, or activities at school?

Yes/no/not sure

✤ If yes, what did you learn? *(open-ended)*

✤ What do you think our school could do to make sure everyone feels safe, happy, and welcome? *(open-ended)*

✤ Is there anything else you would like to tell us about how we can make school better for everyone? *(open-ended)*

Example parent/carer survey

We are committed to creating a school environment where every family and child feels safe, respected, and included. This survey is anonymous, and your honest feedback will help us to improve.

+ How confident are you that our school supports children from all types of families (e.g. single parents, same-sex parents, foster families)?

  Scale: very confident, somewhat confident, neutral, not very confident, not confident at all

+ Have you seen or heard about activities, lessons, or resources in our school that celebrate different types of families?

  Yes/no/not sure

+ If yes, what have you seen or heard? *(open-ended)*

+ Do you feel that our school does enough to address bullying, including bullying related to family diversity or gender/sexual identity?

  Scale: very satisfied, satisfied, neutral, dissatisfied, very dissatisfied

+ Please explain your answer. *(open-ended)*

+ Has your child ever shared that they or someone they know has experienced bullying related to family diversity, gender, or sexuality?

  Yes/no/not sure

+ If yes, how was the situation handled, and do you feel it was resolved effectively? *(open-ended)*

+ Have you ever heard your child mention the word 'gay' being used in an unkind or bullying way at school?

  Yes/no/not sure

+ If yes, how do you feel the school should address this? *(open-ended)*

✦ Do you feel confident that staff at our school are knowledgeable about and comfortable addressing issues related to LGBTQ+ inclusion?

Scale: very confident, somewhat confident, neutral, not very confident, not confident at all

✦ Do you believe that our school creates a welcoming environment for all families, regardless of their structure or background?

Scale: strongly agree, agree, neutral, disagree, strongly disagree

✦ Why do you feel this way? *(open-ended)*

✦ Do you think that the school keeps you informed on how the curriculum is LGBTQ+ inclusive?

Scale: strongly agree, agree, neutral, disagree, strongly disagree

✦ Why do you feel this way? *(open-ended)*

✦ (Secondary only) Do you think that the school's relationships and sex education is inclusive of all pupils and equips them for healthy and happy lives?

Scale: strongly agree, agree, neutral, disagree, strongly disagree, don't know

✦ Why do you feel this way? *(open-ended)*

✦ What could the school do to make sure all families and children feel safe, respected, and included? *(open-ended)*

✦ Is there anything else you would like to share about your child's experiences or your thoughts on this matter? *(open-ended)*

Planning tools

Inclusive books

Focus area	Books you have	Books you need	Notes
Diverse families			
Gender stereotypes			
Religion			
Visible disabilities			
Non-visible disabilities			
Race			

Role models

Focus level	People	Events	Places
Intrapersonal			
Interpersonal			
Societal			
Global			

Inclusion planning template

	Autumn term	Winter term	Spring term	Summer term
Vision				
Policy				
Pastoral				
Provision				
Representation and role models				
Community				

Helpful organisations

LGBTQ+ inclusion in education

More Than Flags and Rainbows: Workshops and resources aimed at reducing bullying and promoting LGBTQ+ inclusion in schools: www.morethanflagsandrainbows.com

Diversity Role Models: A charity working to embed inclusion and tackle LGBTQ+ bullying in schools through educational workshops: www.diversityrolemodels.org

Diverse Educators: Training and resources for a wide range of areas of diversity: www.diverseeducators.co.uk

Proud Trust: Offers resources, advice, and training for creating an LGBTQ+ inclusive environment including setting up LGBTQ+ clubs and events: www.theproudtrust.org

Schools Out: An LGBT+ charity supporting LGBT+ people through education, advocacy, and events such as LGBT+ History Month: https://lgbtplushistorymonth.co.uk

Sex Education Forum: Resources and guidance on inclusive RSE and sex education: www.sexeducationforum.org.uk/

Mental health and well-being

MindOut: A mental health charity run by and for LGBTQ+ people with resources useful for supporting LGBTQ+ pupils: https://mind-out.org.uk

Place2Be: Information and resources for schools to support mental health and inclusivity: www.place2be.org.uk

Young Minds: Offers support on mental health issues impacting LGBTQ+ youth with resources for teachers and parents: www.youngminds.org.uk

Addressing bullying and discrimination

Anti-Bullying Alliance: Guidance on tackling homophobic, biphobic, and transphobic bullying in schools: https://anti-bullyingalliance.org.uk

Childline: Offers information and support for children experiencing bullying which can be shared with pupils: www.childline.org.uk

Kick It Out: Resources on combating discrimination, especially useful for schools tackling anti-LGBTQ+ language in sports: www.kickitout.org

Support for parents and families

Families and Friends of Lesbians and Gays (FFLAG): Resources to support parents in understanding and accepting their LGBTQ+ children: www.fflag.org.uk

Proud 2 b Parents: Support for LGBTQ+ parents and carers as well as for parents of LGBTQ+ children: www.proud2bparents.co.uk

Policies and legal guidance

Equality and Human Rights Commission (EHRC): Guidance on discrimination law, including the rights of LGBTQ+ pupils in school settings: www.equalityhumanrights.com

Government Equalities Office – Guidance for Schools: Official resources to understand school obligations under the Equality Act 2010: https://www.gov.uk/government/publications/equality-act-2010-advice-for-schools

RSE guidance for each UK nation

England: *Relationships Education, Relationships and Sex Education (RSE) and Health Education*: https://www.gov.uk/government/publications/relationships-education-relationships-and-sex-education-rse-and-health-education

Northern Ireland: *Relationships and Sexuality Education (RSE)*: https://www.education-ni.gov.uk/articles/relationship-and-sexuality-education-rse

Scotland: *Guidance on the Delivery of Relationships, Sexual Health and Parenthood (RSHP) Education*: https://rshp.scot

Wales: *Curriculum for Wales: Relationships and Sexuality Education (RSE) Code*: https://www.gov.wales/curriculum-wales-relationships-and-sexuality-education-rse-code

Further reading and professional development

Diverse Book List by More Than Flags and Rainbows: A curated list of fiction and non-fiction books promoting LGBTQ+ awareness across different age groups, available to support inclusive reading in classrooms and libraries: https://www.morethanflagsandrainbows.com/diverse-book-list

Pride & Progress: Podcast, resources, support, and networking for LGBTQ+ teachers: www.prideprogress.co.uk

References

Buchanan, D. and Huczynski, A. (2019). *Organizational Behaviour: An Introductory Text*, 9th edn (Harlow: Pearson).

Cacciapuoti, A. (2016). *Baking with Dad* (London: Child's Play International).

Congress.gov (2019). H.R.5 – 116th Congress (2019–2020): Equality Act (20 May). Available at: https://www.congress.gov/116/bills/hr5/BILLS-116hr5rfs.pdf.

Department for Education (2019). *Relationships Education, Relationships and Sex Education (RSE) and Health Education: Statutory Guidance for Governing Bodies, Proprietors, Head Teachers, Principals, Senior Leadership Teams, Teachers*. Available at: https://www.gov.uk/government/publications/relationships-education-relationships-and-sex-education-rse-and-health-education.

Department for Education and Zahawi, N. (2022). Political Impartiality in Schools (17 February). Available at: https://www.gov.uk/government/publications/political-impartiality-in-schools.

Eagleton, I. (1991). *Ned and the Lonely Fisherman* (Leamington Spa: Owlet Press).

Gilbert, I. (2007). *The Little Book of Thunks: 260 Questions to Make Your Brain Go Ouch!* (Carmarthen: Crown House Publishing).

Goldby, M. (2023). A Note on the Term 'Queer', *Museum of Croydon* [blog]. Available at: https://museumofcroydon.com/blogs-queer-croydon/blog-post-title-two-nl5fj.

Halbert, J. and Kaser, L. (2017). *Leading Through Spirals of Inquiry: For Equity and Quality* (Winnipeg: Portage & Main Press).

Hall, R., Taylor, J., Hewitt, C. E., Heathcote, C., Jarvis, S. W., Langton, T. and Fraser, L. (2024). Impact of Social Transition in Relation to Gender for Children and Adolescents: A Systematic Review, *Archives of Disease in Childhood*, 109: s12–s18. Available at: https://adc.bmj.com/content/109/Suppl_2/s12.

Han, E. and O'Mahoney, J. (2014). British Colonialism and the Criminalization of Homosexuality, *Cambridge Review of International Affairs*, 27(2): 268–288. Available at: https://doi.org/10.1080/09557571.2013.867298.

Hannon, V. and Peterson, A. (2021). *Thrive: The Purpose of Schools in a Changing World* (Cambridge: Cambridge University Press).

Hubbard, T. K. (2020). Historical Views of Homosexuality: Ancient Greece, *Oxford Research Encyclopedia of Politics*. Available at: https://oxfordre.com/politics/display/10.1093/acrefore/9780190228637.001.0001/acrefore-9780190228637-e-1242.

Iglikowski-Broad, V. (2023). Section 28: Impact, Fightback and Repeal, *National Archives*. Available at: https://beta.nationalarchives.gov.uk/explore-the-collection/stories/section-28-impact-fightback-repeal.

Just Like Us (2021). *Growing Up LGBT+: The Impact of School, Home and Coronavirus on LGBT+ Young People*. Available at: https://www.justlikeus.org/wp-content/uploads/2021/11/Just-Like-Us-2021-report-Growing-Up-LGBT.pdf.

Just Like Us (2023). *Positive Futures: How Supporting LGBT+ Young People Enables Them to Thrive in Adulthood*. Available at: https://www.justlikeus.org/wp-content/uploads/2023/05/Positive-Futures-report-by-Just-Like-Us-compressed-for-mobile.pdf.

Knitting Circle (1989). Section 28 Gleanings. Available at: https://web.archive.org/web/20070818063344/http://www.knittingcircle.org.uk/gleanings2889.html.

Martin, C. L. and Ruble, D. N. (2010). Patterns of Gender Development, *Annual Review of Psychology*, 61: 353–381. Available at: https://doi.org/10.1146/annurev.psych.093008.100511.

Moyano, N. and Sánchez-Fuentes, M. d. M. (2020). Homophobic Bullying at Schools: A Systematic Review of Research, Prevalence, School-Related Predictors and Consequences, *Aggression and Violent Behavior*, 53: 101441. Available at: https://doi.org/10.1016/j.avb.2020.101441.

Office for National Statistics (2023a). Sexual Orientation, England and Wales: Census 2021 (6 January). Available at: https://www.ons.gov.uk/peoplepopulationandcommunity/culturalidentity/sexuality/bulletins/sexualorientationenglandandwales/census2021.

Office for National Statistics (2023b). Sexual Orientation, UK: 2021 and 2022 (27 September). Available at: https://www.ons.gov.uk/peoplepopulationandcommunity/culturalidentity/sexuality/bulletins/sexualidentityuk/2021and2022.

Pearce, T. (2020). LGBT Representation on TV Through the Ages – from *Eastenders'* First Gay Kiss to Transgender Superheroes, *Metro* (24 June). Available at: https://metro.co.uk/2020/06/24/lgbt-representation-tv-major-moments-12894718.

Robertson, C. (2014). *Two Dads: A Book About Adoption* (N.p.: Sparklypoo Publications).

Scottish Government (2023). *Delivery of Relationships, Sexual Health and Parenthood Education in Scottish Schools: Draft Guidance* (24 August). Available at: https://www.gov.scot/publications/guidance-delivery-relationships-sexual-health-parenthood-rshp-education-scottish-schools/pages/3/.

Sex Education Forum (2024). *Young People's RSE Poll 2024* (11 April). Available at: https://www.sexeducationforum.org.uk/sites/default/files/field/attachment/Young%20Peoples%20RSE%20Poll%202024%20-%20Report.pdf.

Sinek, S. (2009). *Start with Why: How Great Leaders Inspire Everyone to Take Action* (New York: Penguin).

The Trevor Project (2023). *2023 U.S. National Survey on the Mental Health of LGBTQ Young People*. Available at: https://www.thetrevorproject.org/survey-2023/assets/static/05_TREVOR05_2023survey.pdf.